STANDING FOR SOMETHING

MARK SEDDON

STANDING FOR SOMETHING

Life in the Awkward Squad

Foreword and cartoons by
MARTIN ROWSON

Biteback Publishing

First published in 2011 by
Biteback Publishing
Westminster Tower
10th floor, 3 Albert Embankment
London
SE1 7SP

www.bitebackpublishing.com

ISBN 978-1-84954-123-7

10 9 8 7 6 5 4 3 2 1

A CIP catalogue record for this book is available from the British Library.

Set in Minion Pro by Soapbox
Cover design by Namkwan Cho

Printed and bound in Great Britain by
TJ Interntional, Padstow, Cornwall

Contents

Foreword

IT'S OFTEN BEEN said of my old friend Mark Seddon that we were due to establish full socialism in this country on a Thursday afternoon in October 1998 – except that Mark was organising it and forgot, because he was still having lunch at the Gay Hussar, that fabled watering hole of the Left in Greek Street, Soho. Actually, I'm the one who's said that, many times, but it never seems to have bothered him much. Indeed, one of Mark's more endearing qualities is his capacity for optimism and staying remarkably jolly, given the circumstances.

After all, in less sordid times than those he describes in this book, Mark would probably have been an MP for getting on for a decade and a half by now. As it is, the Blairite faction of the Permanent Institutionalised Thatcherite Revolutionary Party (or New Labour, as it was commonly known) marked him down with the Black Spot, so we'll never know what he might have achieved in the mainstream of politics, in the heart of the Westminster beast. Or failed to have achieved, for that matter. And as there are two occasions when Mark's timidity prevented the steady onward course of New Labour from being seriously disturbed, maybe it's better not to speculate too deeply on that unknowable, alternative glittering career.

Mark refers in this book to the first occasion, but to put the record straight I'll give my version, which differs in several key areas from his. The occasion when I proposed soiling Blair's bog was a different conference from the one where I proposed to David Yelland, editor of the *Sun*, that I draw the Twin Towers on the back of his head as a tribute to 9/11. That was in Blackpool in 2001; the Blair's bog incident was in Bournemouth in 1998, when Seddon, Nyta Mann, Bill Hagerty and I were taking a shortcut from one side of town to the other through the Conference Centre and its surrounding Ring of Steel. Having got in, Mark thought he'd show off his status as a member of the NEC by giving us a backstage tour. We did indeed poke around Blair's dressing room and admire his fruit basket and the mirror with the light bulbs, but my proposal to have a dump in his khazi was far more than mere scatology. My plan, in fact, was for all four of us, having just had a curry, to have a crap, like shitty Spartacuses, and *then not flush the toilet*, merely in order to see how the world's media would cover with good taste this shocking breach of the Prime Minister's security.

It never happened, obviously, and if it had it probably wouldn't have made much of a splash, so to speak. However, a few years earlier Mark, if he'd followed my advice, could have strangled New Labour at birth. It was at the Special One-Day Conference to kill off Clause Four at the Methodist Central Hall in Spring 1995. Mark and I were sitting in the circle, just behind Richard Attenborough (a Labour peer), when we spotted Alastair Campbell hunched over his laptop a few yards away, overlooking the stage from the edge of the balcony. I did a brief recce, and established that he was doing a last-minute run-through of the text of Blair's keynote speech to rip the soul of socialism out of the Labour Party, so I suggested to

Mark that he go over and say hello, as Campbell was then a regular contributor to *Tribune*.

But I suggested that Mark should also, as he patted Campbell on the back in convivial greeting, at the same time accidentally-on-purpose press the 'delete' key on Campbell's keyboard. Needless to say, Mark chickened out, and so the sight of Blair staring in growing panic at his blank plastic dummy boards, the pathetic spectacle of him stuttering and mouthing soundlessly rousing the party to nip Blairism in the bud, will remain for ever one of history's What Might Have Beens. (As must what might have happened later that day, when fellow *Guardian* cartoonist Steve Bell and I followed Blair and his entourage backstage to the post-conference cast party, where I nearly blagged our way in before Steve confessed to the attendant Millbank spokeschild that our presence was entirely unauthorised.)

We can, and probably should, blame Mark for these two non-events, though it seems a bit churlish, and he's certainly acquitted himself in other ways in his many adventures, as you'll find out when you read this book. Which brings me back to his optimism.

I, like Mark, witnessed the rise and fall of New Labour, itself just another sorry chapter in our nation's history of craven surrender to wealth, power and the complacency that bolster both. Mark's response was altogether more proactive than mine, which was to rip the piss out of the monster, laughing in order to cover my tears of despair. Mark, on the other hand, always maintained his good spirits, and was able, at least for a part of the time, to make our act of witness to the unfolding horror story thoroughly, if revoltingly, enjoyable. So I'm grateful for that, and for all those truly weird evenings upstairs in the Gay Hussar, and even for him browbeating me into doing my Martin Bell impression at the 1997 Tribune Rally – although he announced me an hour later than he said he would, all of which time I'd been in the venue's bar, working (and drinking) on the basis that I was surplus to requirements. I still wake up now and again in a cold sweat at the memory of that evening, though when I reminded Mark about the details (which he'd conveniently forgotten), he just laughed.

As, I hope, will you, even if the real reason behind Mark Seddon's jollity is because the rumours that have been bandied round the Gay Hussar for the last twenty years are true, and he really *is* working for MI5.

Martin Rowson
Lewisham, August 2011

Preface

HISTORY, IT IS said, tends to be written by the victors. In a British context this could partly explain why publishers are increasingly reluctant to publish books deemed 'political'. This is because they are largely boring. And this is because most of the political 'victors' of our times are simply, well, boring individuals. Just think of all of those swiftly remaindered biographies of former government ministers! And be honest, would you really want to share a pint with Tony Blair or David Cameron?

All of which may partly explain why it has taken so long for this book to see the light of day. I owe special thanks to Gill Coleridge of Coleridge, Rogers and White, who first saw the merit in what I proposed several years back, even as we received a number of knockbacks from publishers – or rather the bean-counters in their accounts departments – who all said, 'Not yet another "New" Labour memoir!' As I do to Jo Phillips, who first suggested I write it.

David Miller took up where Gill left off after my return from New York, where I had spent over two years setting up the New York Bureau of Al Jazeera and working as its United Nations correspondent, and it is thanks to him, to Sean Magee, and to my old sparring partner Iain Dale of Biteback Publishing that *Standing for Something* finally makes this appearance. Of course, it would be remiss of me not to mention my old friend and lunching companion of two decades Martin Rowson, whose illustrations grace this tome, as they do our other front room, the Gay Hussar restaurant in Soho, London, as well as innumerable newspapers and magazines.

When I began writing, Tony Blair was Prime Minister and New Labour seemed impregnable. The party in government had achieved the previously unthinkable in aligning itself to the neo-liberal, free-market policies of the previous Conservative governments. Labour Ministers were paying their respects to the City of London, and attacking excessive red tape, while the grip of an increasingly monopolised, popular tabloid culture stifled debate and intimidated many who might otherwise have challenged the power of the media barons. Lest we forget, during this period Tony Blair had talked of the 'scars on my back', while moaning about the public services to the British Venture Capitalist Association. When no weapons of mass destruction could be found in Iraq, Blair told the Labour Party Conference, 'I only know what I believe.' It was the late and lamented Robin Cook who saved us from worse; intervening to stop Blair from saying 'I am proud of the British Empire!' in a planned foreign policy speech prior to the 1997 General Election.

It is staggering to think that grown men and women regarded so much of this doggerel with a mixture of awe and wonderment. Here are just a few of the New Labour homilies we had to endure, Orwellian 'doublespeak' for the most part, such as; 'earned autonomy', 'blue sky thinking', 'constructive ambiguity', 'margin for prudence', 'coalitions of the willing', 'rights and responsibilities', 'new localism', 'old Europe', 'light touch regulation', thinking the unthinkable'. My own favourite was an Alan Milburn construct, 'Forward, not back.' Only someone like Milburn would not have known that this hideous homily was once the property of the SED, the Communist party of the old 'German Democratic Republic'. But the list goes on and on ...

As I write this, much of what appeared so permanent is in the process of unravelling. Britain's rotten banking and corporate culture has exploded, as have some of our English inner cities, while Parliament has been buffeted by seemingly endless, grubby expense scandals with some MPs going to jail. On top of that – and perhaps most unexpected of all – the Murdoch empire has begun to unravel. The rotten underbelly of the new English establishment, the flotsam of Murdochracy (the playwright and socialist Dennis Potter famously named his cancer 'Rupert'), the spinners, PR gurus and lightweight politicians have finally been seen for what they all are. At one level I am proud of providing some early warnings of what was to come in the Blair years; at another, deeply disappointed that we have been so ill served by an establishment of spivs for so long.

What I set out to do here is try and make some sense of the Blair years, from the inside track, but increasingly as an outsider looking in. But I also revisit more elevating and interesting times spent a foreign TV reporter, occupying that wonderful ringside seat on life that can be afforded to journalists.

Standing for Something is dedicated to all of those who try to make a difference, who question, who dissent and who are fully signed up members of the awkward squad. In particular, this book is dedicated to my former colleagues at the Al Jazeera English TV Network, especially the pioneers who were there at the start of one of the greatest media experiments of our time – and one that is unlikely to be repeated again on such an epic scale. In doing so,

I would like to single out my immediate former colleagues in the New York Bureau, Kristen Saloomey, Nick Castellaro and Melorine Mokri, the best people I have had the privilege of working with in over twenty years in print and broadcast television. To sign up for the Al Jazeera Network in America when the neo-cons were in their pomp goes beyond the normal call of journalistic duty, especially if you were American, as Kristen and Melorine are.

And so to friends in America and in Britain who have at different times provided much needed friendship and inspiration: Ian Williams and Anora Mahmudova, Jennifer Jessup, David Lansbury, Chantal Ribeiro, Kieran Baker, Reg Oberlag, Giorgio Gomelsky, Don Peebles, Peter Gerry, Karina Huber, Jeff Gold, John Mason, Andy Darmoo, John Cryer, Steve Clark, Jenny Stringer, John and Henrietta Goelet, Jay Chavda, Michael Meacher, Jo Phillips, Bill Hagerty, Nyta Mann, Andrew Neil, John Cummings, Glyn Ford, Grahame Morris, Hugh MacPherson, Pete Willsman, Tim Pendry, Geoffrey Goodman and others too many to mention.

To them my thanks, and above all to my family – Yasmin, Matthew and Saffron in particular – who have had to put up with the perennial difficulties of living with a restless spirit. And not forgetting my father and mother, Tony and Hilary, who provided us three – Joanne, Paul and me – with a moral compass.

Mark Seddon
August 2011

Introduction

THE TIME HAS come for yet another memoir by a former Labour insider, detailing *ad nauseam* the tiffs and tantrums of Messrs Blair, Brown and Mandelson. Actually that is neither what I am, nor the story I tell here. I am a journalist and campaigner – an outsider who spent much of the Blair/Brown years as a reluctant participant inside what became 'New' Labour, before finally fleeing to New York after the war on Iraq in despair, to set up Al Jazeera English TV's new bureau in the city and become the new TV Networks' United Nations Correspondent. I returned to Britain a few years later to discover that very little had changed.

Standing for Something is not yet another Andrew Rawnsley-style account of the intricacies – and irrelevancies – of the dank Blair/Brown/Mandelson Tudor Court. It will not preoccupy itself with the 'Westminster bubble' or what has become known as the 'Westminster beltway' of professional politicians and cheerleading hacks, many of whom delight in the parochialism and trivia that has helped stifle democratic discourse in this country. This has created a new generation of professional politicians, automatons, who dance on a penny, spouting on meaninglessly about 'values' and courted by all too many media lap-dogs, latter-day stenographers, who now wonder why we don't buy their newspapers or watch or listen to their dull programmes. I believe what people really want are politicians and leaders with real principles and convictions, prepared to stand up for them and argue for them. Love them or loathe them, you can't accuse Margaret Thatcher or Dennis Skinner of not standing for something; nor Alex Salmond, David Davis, Bob Crow or Ann Widdecombe for that matter. The sad truth is that today's political class largely lacks empathy; most politicians no longer know how to relate to people and speak their language. They lack the common touch, because the conveyor belt that takes them from student hackery to MP's researcher and then to Parliament means that fewer of them have ever had real jobs. Just think of Tony Blair, David Cameron and George Osborne; none of them ever had a real job outside politics. There is nothing to celebrate in the fact that public disinterest in politics has grown along with a deep and corrosive cynicism, also fed by sections of the media. The expenses scandal crossed a new Rubicon. In the early part of the twenty-first century, the political class was not just widely derided, it was actively disliked. Joining them were the bankers and speculators who had succeeding in trashing the British economy, and the icing on the cake was provided by the Murdoch media, which had managed to cast its baleful spell over the political class to such an extent that by the time David Cameron scraped in as Prime Minister, News Corporation more or less 'owned' him.

Standing for Something finally opens the lid on the New Labour years, casting light into dark places. It reveals new information on what went on behind the scenes in the build-up to the Iraq War, which has subsequently been sent to the Chilcot Inquiry.

It also presents a number of closely observed political portraits, not only of leading lights in the Labour Party, but of Conservatives, press barons, celebrities and foreign leaders, all of whom the author came to know, interviewed or worked with over the past decade. This is a 'warts and all' exposé of what it is really like as an outsider on the inside during Tony Blair's rise to power – and during it – as well as a period spent operating on an altogether broader canvas, at the United Nations in New York and from many different trouble spots and countries around the world.

There are stand-alone portraits and numerous vignettes, some flattering, others not, compiled in a style familiar to anyone who has had a stint as a Fleet Street diarist, including this author. The cast of characters includes the following: Tony Blair, Gordon Brown, Peter Mandelson and Alastair Campbell, who have been deified and damned in equal measure; Rupert Murdoch, Rebekah Brooks, Michael Foot, Barbara Castle, Tony Benn, Ken Livingstone, Ken Clarke, John Bercow, trade union leaders Arthur Scargill and Bob Crow, David Blunkett, Neil Kinnock, John Prescott, George Galloway, Iain Duncan Smith, John Smith, Mo Mowlam, Clare Short, Paul Foot, Piers Morgan, John Major, Denis Healey, Charles Moore, Dennis Skinner, Andrew Neil, and the late Lord Rothermere and Sir James Goldsmith.

What really went on behind the scenes with Blair, Mandelson and Brown? How did they crush internal opposition, undermine the Labour Conference, and replace policy and principle with soundbites? What role did Labour's ruling National Executive Committee (NEC) and the unions play in rubber-stamping and closing Labour down as a political movement? And what of the media? What role did journalists, newspapers and television play in helping to sustain the Blair 'New' Labour brand? What really happened behind the scenes in the run up to the war in Iraq, and what did Tony Blair tell the author from the Downing Street sofa?

What happened when Rupert Murdoch came to call, and what were the real Gordon Brown and John Prescott like? How did the control freaks do for Ken Livingstone? With power increasingly centralised, what role did the secretive Joint Policy Commission and Economic Policy Commission play? And what happened to those who didn't play ball in the years of 'Command and Control'? From Blair's first strike at dissidents in the European Labour Party to the endgame of centrally picked, 'parachuted in' Parliamentary candidates, this is the story that Andrew Rawnsley and others didn't tell, because they couldn't tell it. They weren't there.

How have our democracy and our civil liberties been curtailed, and is there any answer to the superficial, dumbed-down apology for a Parliament that we have today? Does one of Labour's worst ever General Election defeats and the election of a new leader mean that anything will finally begin to change?

Standing for Something begins with the premise that little really changes in Britain, except that the political establishment becomes better skilled at persuading us that it does. This will be a book that seeks to reveal the truth about a new power elite in Britain. It called itself 'New Labour' and rapidly became driven by authoritarian reflexes. It squandered the best opportunity since the ending of the Second War to bring in profound economic and social reform that could have made Britain a more prosperous and equal country. This is an account then of how Tony Blair and Gordon Brown essentially maintained the old Thatcherite consensus, and how Labour was transformed from being a force for liberal social democracy to one of illiberal neo-conservatism, and one that also threw in its lot with America's disastrous wars in Afghanistan and Iraq. An historic opportunity was lost when that 1997 General Election produced a huge majority for Tony Blair and for Labour, an opportunity to transform Britain economically and socially. But then we know that neither Blair nor Brown thought they would be given such a large majority in Parliament. For his part, Blair didn't want it – and would have preferred to have reached a deal with Paddy Ashdown and the Liberal Democrats. Instead, Tony Blair and his New Labour project acted only on inherited policies from Neil Kinnock and John Smith, such as devolution and the minimum wage, but as time progressed, essentially continued the neo-liberal economic project that had been Britain's lot since the end of the 1970s. That project essentially allowed the rich to get richer, and the poor to get poorer. Britain's two-tier economy – the super-rich and the rest – remained unchallenged, and then the country's casino economy burst like a bubble.

A few of us had already concluded that this was the direction Blair would take Labour and the country in soon after he became Labour leader, which is why when others were celebrating Labour's famous win in May 1997, three of us – cartoonist Martin Rowson, the journalist, Nyta Mann and myself – were huddled in the Gay Hussar restaurant in Soho, next to a large mock-up of the famous 1945 'Labour in Power' *Daily Herald* front page, pessimistically pondering what would come next. Part of me was excited – who wouldn't be after all of those long years in opposition? But an early signal as to how Blair and his entourage intended playing things came as footage of the new PM sweeping into Downing Street past adoring crowds was shown later that afternoon. The BBC claimed that the Union Jack-waving crowd was spontaneous. Looking around, though, I could see very many familiar faces. While you could not fault New Labour's efficient PR machine, was it really necessary to bus in loads of party officials to wave Union Jacks?

So *Standing for Something* is a deeply personal account of how a youthful attachment to principle survived well into adulthood and how an abiding naiveté about the real nature of power and the corruption of power blinded me to the baser motives of many of those who had grabbed it. The book charts my passage as editor of the left-wing weekly *Tribune* to elected member of Labour's ruling National Executive Committee, to my attempts to get selected as a Labour candidate, along with the repeated attempts by the party machine to prevent, crush and drive out those like me who didn't 'follow the line'.

Above all, *Standing for Something* is an account of a political journey and the fight for principle at a time when Tony Blair, Peter Mandelson and their close supporters in politics and much of the commentariat were determined to rewrite the history books and consign the Labour Party as a force for social democracy into the dustbin. In this, they may have partially failed – but their poisoned legacy lives on, encapsulated in a very special and deep contempt felt by many for the British political class as a whole. What followed New Labour was a coalition government dominated by the Conservatives, who were intent to privatise whatever was left of Britain's public services, and under the guise of 'reform' intended to cut expenditure and continue the shift of power and wealth from those who largely don't have it to those who largely do.

But this is more than a tale of a parochial, tired country, grown weary with a political class that had become venal and corrupt. *Standing for Something* is also an account of my experience as a foreign correspondent, based in New York at the United Nations; an opportunity to observe and report from a larger global canvas and to put the British political scene into some sort of context.

Standing for Something will take the reader away from the machinations of the New Labour years to pre-war Iraq and a chance interview with Tariq Aziz; to North Africa and Palestine with Yasser Arafat; to Pyongyang with Kim Jong Il; to Africa with the new UN Secretary General, Ban Ki-Moon; to Gdansk to meet Lech Walesa; and to the Bronx on the trail of Hugo Chavez. There are close portraits of some of those the author came to know or to interview in New York, including actor George Clooney and the radical musician and former Rolling Stones and Animals manager, Giorgio Gomelsky, as well as the relationship the author struck up with actress and campaigner Mia Farrow. Other characters include US billionaire Jim Chanos, short-trader and buster of Enron, as well as some chance encounters with George Bush's UN Ambassador, the neo-con John Bolton, and Senator John McCain.

Awakening

I WAS INTERESTED in politics well before I was a teenager or a student. I could only have been about eleven or twelve when the National Union of Mineworkers, then led by Joe Gormley, called a strike for better pay and conditions. In the early part of 1974 the lights kept on going out at my boarding school in Camberley, Surrey. (My father was an Army officer, and at the time my parents had been posted to Northern Ireland.) One evening the headmaster, a Mr Haggard, stood before us all at supper and solemnly announced that there would be no more power cuts that evening – at which point all the lights went out.

Edward Heath called a General Election that year, demanding an answer to the question, 'Who Governs Britain?' – to which voters emphatically answered, 'Not you!' I remember being fascinated by the stand-off and the power that the miners seemed to have, as well as the excitement of patrolling the freezing school corridors with candles. And when it came to that election, a group of us were sent out to gauge public opinion in the village of Crowthorne in Surrey, which I dimly recall showed one Enoch Powell leading in the popularity stakes. Since everybody else at school seemed to be Tory, I opted to support Plaid Cymru, and began an occasional correspondence with the late Gwynfor Evans, then leader of Plaid – and one of Welsh Nationalism's heroes. Evans didn't seem to mind writing back to a precocious prep school boy without a drop of Welsh blood in his body – far from it, he encouraged me to learn Welsh. So that is why I came to know that 'Nerthi Gymru', means 'Power for Wales'.

I have had a lifetime aversion to sporting activity of any kind. Instead, I was into gardening. At the age of twelve, with my friend James Stewart, we made a discovery of a long abandoned walled garden, replete with ornamental pond, that had once stood in the grounds of the long-demolished Edgebarrow Manor, near Crowthorne, not far from the school boundaries. This was our regular escape – a den that was only known to us and to an elderly lady, Mrs Christie , who lived on her own in isolated Rosina Cottage just above the bamboo and rhododendron thickets. Her brother was Walter Johnson, the Labour MP for Derby South who was later to become infamous for attacking Michael Foot for 'dressing like a navvy' at the Cenotaph when Foot was leader of the party. Michael and Jill were very upset by this at the time, as Jill told me years later: 'It was a brand new coat, bought from Jaeger, which the Queen Mother had commended Michael on. She said "Michael, it's just the right sort of coat for this rather inclement weather."'

But it was Walter Johnson, hardly a Labour firebrand, and an MP who is probably only now remembered for his savaging of Michael's coat, who really got me hooked. He took my friend Charlie Crole and me around Parliament and onto the terrace, and that was it.

I managed to scrape into a minor public school, Dauntsey's School in Wiltshire – a disappointment to my parents, who had hoped that I might make Wellington College in Berkshire – and joined the Labour Party at fifteen, having written to James Callaghan the year before asking if I could do so. I had also received a letter from the South West Region of the party, saying I was 'too young' to join and must wait a year. I remember being called in to the Headmaster's study by Guy King Reynolds, who declared, 'My friend Kate Gillington says you want to join the Labour Party – and it is all absolutely fine by her and the others.' Kate Gillington knew my headmaster from the Magistrates' Court in Devizes, where they both served. The contrast between the attitude of my headmaster and the rest of my family who were frankly horrified is something that has never entirely left me. But once a month for the next two or three years, I would get a lift into Devizes with a retired bank manager who was also a member of the Devizes Labour Party for the regular branch meetings. These branch meetings were an early introduction to how politics worked at a very local level. For although the Devizes constituency traditionally sent a Conservative MP to Parliament, back in the 1970s there was an active Labour culture in some of the market towns. I suppose our group of members was a fairly typical cross-section of the community. There were a couple of retirees, one of whom had worked on the land, and then there was a particularly angry middle-aged National Union of Public Employees official from the local hospital. Margaret and Ray Taylor were both teachers and probably the most active, since Margaret tended to volunteer to go to the Labour conference each year. Her hero was a young Labour Minister with a bright future ahead of him: one Neil Kinnock. It was probably at their instigation that I got invited to listen to Neil in full oratorical flow at a meeting of the Marlborough College Fabian Society. For those who have never heard Neil Kinnock – the unconstrained real Neil Kinnock – delivering a speech, the only other contemporary Welsh radical who could come anywhere near is Tyrone O'Sullivan, the redoubtable leader of the Tower Colliery miners' co-operative. As Kinnock finished taking questions, Margaret Taylor took me over to meet him. To this day I remember being tongue-tied – not a problem that was ever visited on Neil.

I managed to get a visitor's ticket to the 1978 Labour Party Conference in Brighton, since my grandparents lived there, and back then all you had to do was walk into the conference centre, where there wasn't a policeman in sight, and ask for a ticket. This of course was at the fag-end of the Labour government, but I was able to recognise many of the faces on the platform – not least because many of them featured in my family's lexicon of distaste: Clive Jenkins, Joan Maynard, Tony Benn, Frank Allaun, Ian Mikardo, Eric Heffer and Barbara Castle. My grandfather Dennis had worked for the Post Office in Brighton and remembered helping another Dennis – Dennis Hobson, the Brighton postman – win his Kemptown seat at the 1945 election. In later life, my grandfather ended up voting for the National Front. My grandmother Vera really didn't have much time for all of the Labour people – in fact she positively disliked many of them, recounting tales of drunkenness in conference hotels. I'm fairly sure she voted for the National Front in one election as well – which could of course be connected to the fact that the then putative British Fuhrer, John Tyndall, lived in the next street to them in Hove. From time to time, therefore, they would meet him at the bus stop.

But looking back, the varied backgrounds, politics and experience of a cast of characters such as most of the above leaves most of today's intake standing on the sidelines. Back then Labour was a real political movement, where passionate debate and disagreement were part and parcel of what it was all about.

Tremendous debates took place at the autumn conferences, and resolutions were voted on, which sometimes could not be ignored by Labour Ministers. The National Executive Committee was a power in the land in itself, responsible for a range of powerful policy-making committees. And back then you could be sure that policy-making was largely free of the cancer of corporate lobbying and control. By the end of the Blair New Labour interregnum, the NEC was largely gutted of any political role, policy was largely decided by Blair, Brown and Mandelson, and the conference reduced to a hideously stage-managed charade infested by lobbyists, PR companies and the rest of the flotsam that attaches itself to politics and power. How many people are aware that party conferences are increasingly full of business people rather than members, or that the conference hall is ritually packed out by those who have corporate stalls, because there simply aren't enough members to fill the space? The Conservative Party is similarly de-populated of members. Of the 12,000-odd people who attended the last Conservative Conference, barely 2,500 were actually members of the party.

No one dares tell the truth that Britain's political parties are parties in name only. Membership has slumped over the past thirty years, and by the time Labour lost office in May 2010, the average membership in some of the strongest Labour constituencies was around 300, many retired or elderly. Following the 2010 General Election, Labour did begin to attract back some members, but without the 'affiliated members' in the unions, the party membership remained a feeble shadow of its former self.

At that Labour Conference in 1978 Margaret Taylor introduced me to Norman Lake, who was a Labour councillor in Norwich – and since I had just managed to get a place at the University of East Anglia to read Development Studies, it was good to be able to meet someone from the city I had never even been to. Norman told me to get myself down to the Labour Club in Bethel Street one Saturday and he would introduce me to some of the members. Norwich had a fine radical tradition that stretched all the way back to the Peasants' Revolt, the early attempts to form workers' societies by the shoemakers, and of course support for the French Revolution; and the city was sufficiently isolated to be something of an independent oasis of radicalism amidst the blue sea of East Anglia. In the early 1980s the city's Labour council was justly admired, even by its critics, for a thoughtful municipal socialism, which had particularly transformed the post-war lives of many with excellent housing, sports facilities and parks. Norwich kept on electing Labour councils, as it tended to return Labour MPs. In the early 1980s David Ennals and John Garrett were the city's two MPs. And Norwich City Council became the last line of resistance against Margaret Thatcher's 'right to buy' policy, arguing unsuccessfully in the courts that if councils were forced to sell properties, and at a massive discount, the receipts at least should go back into new build.

I threw myself into local Norwich Labour politics with far more enthusiasm than student politics, even though I was to end up being elected President of the University of East Anglia Students' Union in the years of the miners' strike, 1984. Not only did the Labour Party have its own headquarters with a large meeting hall, the Fraser Hall (opened by Harold Wilson) for the packed General Committee meetings (ninety-odd delegates would attend these each month), there was a bar attached as well. With 2,000 members across the city, an active Trades Council and regular political events and campaigns, the Norwich Labour Party was also something of a social hub. The local Tote was played by thousands across the city and raised funds for the party. There was a real sense of civic pride about the place, which even extended to the decision by Labour councillors to hand over a big chunk of council land on the outskirts of the city for a new university to be built: the University of East Anglia.

The campaign slogan for the Norwich Labour Party would invariably be 'Do Different', which I didn't have much trouble in taking to heart. If the Liberals ever managed to get their hands on one of the council seats near the university, the Labour Party would fight back with gusto, deploying dozens of activists. Elections were taken seriously in Norwich, with a pretty large proportion of homes displaying posters for the different parties, although the colour red would tend to outnumber the others. Such was my keenness to get people to put the posters up during one general election that I was renamed 'Sticker Seddon' by some of the comrades.

I soon became the Chair of the UEA Labour Club, and managed to increase our representation on the Norwich Labour Party General Committee. And with friends I also organised a few sorties by Labour students to go and help in various by-elections – most memorably in Bermondsey, then being fought by Peter Tatchell. Tatchell was in the unfortunate position of having been sort of dropped as a Labour candidate by Michael Foot, being savaged by some of the old mafia who had formed the machine around the previous sitting MP, Bob Mellish, and through being hit by a particularly vicious homophobic campaign. I remember Mellish's agent John O'Grady riding a horse and cart through the then wastelands of the Surrey Docks belting out all sorts vicious little ditties – the running theme being that Tatchell was a draft-dodging Aussie poof. That by-election was of course famously won by one Simon Hughes, who is also gay, but who managed not to utter a single word of condemnation for the vile insults heaped on Tatchell. One day, having got our lot of canvassers into the back of a white Transit van standing in the courtyard of a 1930s tenement, someone shouted, 'Put your foot on it now! There's a fucking fireball heading our way!' Des Hart, the driver, sped off as a burning mass of molten steel came crashing down where the van had been. It was a burning oven, thrown from a top floor – but not at us. Such was the mood surrounding that campaign, our paranoia seemed justified.

I was elected as the Labour Club's candidate for President of the Students' Union at around the same time that miners at Lewis Merthyr Colliery in South Wales were taking part in the first salvoes of what turned out to be the most momentous year for British industrial relations since the ending of the Second World War. As a young student activist I realised that something incredibly serious and final was shaping up, and that this was the stand-off that would enormously affect the political and economic shape of Britain for the foreseeable future. My friend Pat McHale from the Labour Club had taken me 'for your own education' to stay with him, his girlfriend and parents in Maltby in the South Yorkshire coalfield. Pat's father worked at Maltby Colliery, and spending a few days in this archetypal mining community had a lasting effect. I realised that Margaret Thatcher did not appreciate that when she talked of 'family values', 'law and order' and much else, she was talking of places like Maltby, which were incredibly close and supportive communities. In Maltby in the early 1980s, people didn't really see the need to lock their front doors, while in the Miners Welfare Club there was a big notice which read, 'No Swearing'. The clubs, the pubs, the sporting activities, the allotments were all conforming to Mrs Thatcher's slightly perverse idea of what Victorian values might have been. All that might have grated, I suspect, had she and her ilk ever come to somewhere like Maltby, was the propensity of people to be members of the National Union of Mineworkers and to name their roads after people such as Clement Attlee instead of Winston Churchill.

This whole way of life was to face the most enormous upheaval of a year-long struggle to the bitter end by the bulk of Britain's mining communities – although the Nottinghamshire miners, who had objected to not being allowed a national ballot, largely kept working. The miners and their families supported their union out of something far deeper than loyalty, although their union was led, with an intransigence which matched that of Margaret Thatcher, by Arthur Scargill. But that year was to be a year of real education for me, as first we opened the University of East Anglia to miners' pickets who had come down from the Durham coalfield in order to try and block some of the East Anglian small ports from bringing in imported coal. Then I travelled to the coalfields, first to Durham and then regularly to Ollerton in Nottinghamshire, with which Norwich Labour Party had 'twinned'.

The University Conservative Club was at that time led by one Iain Dale, who had a deep attachment to Margaret Thatcher, but who deep down I suspect was much more of a moderate Conservative. I can still see him now, walking through the main university square with his Adidas hold-all and blue jacket and jeans. I had overreached myself by sending Student Union vans packed with collected provisions in the regular weekend convoy to the striking Ollerton miners at their Alamo, Ollerton and Bevercotes Welfare. Iain and his Conservative students were pretty sure that the Students' Union were acting *ultra vires*, and they were right. What followed was an attempt to have me thrown out as union President in a 'no confidence' motion, which by some miracle I managed to see off. I remember Iain saying at the time: 'Oh well done, then. It was nothing personal.' To this day, even though I have usually tended to disagree with him over most issues and was particularly appalled by the role – of which he is extremely proud – of breaking the National Dock Labour scheme, as far as I can make out Iain has remained attached to most of the principles and heroes (and to Maggie in particular) of his student youth.

I returned to Ollerton in 2010. The Welfare Hall, that place of huge pans of steaming baked beans, of parties, rallies and so much more, stood derelict. The Nottinghamshire miners who worked through the strike and were lauded by Margaret Thatcher watched as one by one their pits were shut. The Ollerton of today is quite spruced up and the old colliery site occupied by an alternative energy centre.

I haven't been back to Norwich for years, but for some time kept in touch with many of the people I had worked with and campaigned with. Some years after leaving, I had tried to be nominated as the Labour candidate following John Garrett's decision to retire, but along with others was beaten by Charles Clarke, who had been gifted the membership lists weeks before the rest of us had clapped our eyes on them.

Today the old Labour Club has mostly been demolished and the rest sold off, and the Norwich party meets in one of the city's churches, of which they are quite a few. The membership is a fraction of what it used to be, with a number having left in disgust at the treatment meted out to the formidably popular and energetic former Norwich North MP, Ian Gibson, by the Labour Party, as this perennial rebel became a convenient scapegoat for many of the party's ills around the 2009 expenses scandal. Norwich Labour Party was historically the bellwether for the health of the Labour body as a whole. In recent years it has been on life-support, and as I write is without a Labour MP at all in the city. There are rumours of its recovery, which must be good news. But unless that Labour Party locally and nationally begins to stand for something again, it is pretty difficult to envisage the level of vibrancy, depth and involvement that was once the hallmark of Norwich Labour.

After leaving University, and the Students' Union, I applied for a job as a 'researcher to a Labour MP', and was gobsmacked to be called at my aunt's house in Great Missenden by someone from Jim Callaghan's office. In the mid-1980s there were two Jim Callaghans in the House of Commons, and naturally I expected the caller to have been the Labour backbencher and Middleton MP, James Callaghan. In fact it was the former Prime Minister, who wanted to know when I could go and meet him for an interview.

Once I was settled in his study, he pointed to a framed picture of the Labour Cabinet of the early 1970s. 'Can you name them?', he asked. In the same way the football nerds can recite endless team names or train-spotters can tell you how a Deltic Class locomotive differs from a Pacific Class loco, I knew them all. 'Very good. But you are very young.' He must have seen my disappointment. 'You will just have to get more experience, and how you get that experience is another thing altogether. It's what might be called a Catch-22 question!'

Farewell to Labour – and to 'JP'

THE FIRST MEETING of Labour's National Executive Committee I attended in September 1998 had been in the Imperial Hotel in Blackpool. It was a huge room, with the sun pouring in through large sash windows. Newly elected members were sat deliberately in front of the windows, so that when Tony Blair and his entourage came in we all had to screw up our eyes to see him. This is of course how it happens in *The Godfather*.

The election that year of four left-wingers – including myself (I had won the highest number of votes with a tally of 75,580) – was not supposed to have happened, and the party machine had done its damnedest to stop us. Tony Blair gave us a stern lecture on the need for discipline, and not allowing the media the opportunity to attack the party. Robin Cook, who was leaving the NEC, had come past and whispered 'Good luck' in my ear, as had Clare Short. Then I turned back, squinting at Tony Blair.

Seven years on in 2005 it was time to leave the NEC to head for New York, where I had just been appointed Al Jazeera's first UN and New York correspondent. We had all assembled in a hotel room in Brighton as another bland Labour conference breathed its last. Jack Dromey, a senior official in the Transport and General Workers' Union, seemed genuinely mystified as to why I was leaving, and even suggested that I go and see him to line up some work with the union. It was difficult not to like Jack, since he had political form. When he was going through one of his hirsute on-message periods, I used to like to remind him of the picture of him in the *Tribune* picture archives. There he stands, all bushy bearded in one of those wide-lapelled 1970s jackets, standing next to the then leader of the Yorkshire miners, Arthur Scargill. This was the Grunwick picket line of the mid 1970s, where he and his future wife Harriet had found each other.

At my final NEC meeting, my old comrade Pete Willsman, a veteran of so many battles for democracy within the Labour Party, gave me a commemorative plate depicting an NUM banner that featured Dennis Skinner, which was all a bit surreal as Dennis was standing next to me as I opened the box. And then Tony Blair briefly went round the table thanking each departing member. He came to me and said: 'Well you know, we haven't agreed on much over the years, in fact I don't think we have agreed on anything really at all. But Mark, you have always put your case reasonably and fairly. You will be welcome back.' Given our disagreements, I thought this was pretty decent of him. We each had our pictures taken and were given a certificate. In fact I had collected a number of these NEC certificates, which I suppose was a reward of sorts since I had never taken a brass farthing from the party in expense claims for travel or anything else over the years.

'When are you going to New York?', Blair asked me as we stood for the photographer, and then added: 'Lucky you, and no more NEC meetings either.' He looked a little wistful, mindful of the fact that he had many more NEC meetings in front of him. But then I had always known that Blair found the NEC a bit of a bore, much as I suspect he found Cabinet meetings and probably Parliament a bore too. What may be said in his favour is that, almost uniquely for a former British Prime Minister, he didn't take a peerage on standing down from Parliament. He just went off and made loads of money. Shed loads of money. And as he made more and more money he began to look more and more like the late Liberace, except a rather orange-looking Liberace. It was of course Liberace who coined the phrase that he had 'cried all the way to the bank', after winning a libel case against the *Daily Mirror*.

'So what are you going to do with yer two Jags?', demanded a bristling Prescott from across the table. He and I had never seen eye to eye. But I had once made the error of telling him that I had two Jags as we were waiting for some egg mayonnaise sandwiches at an interlude in a never-ending NEC meeting – not that either car was working. I looked at him and shot back: 'Flog 'em to you, John!'

'JP' had a particular dislike of journalists and from time to time would round on me. On one occasion he pointed at me ferociously during an NEC meeting and said: 'I hate journalists!' Then he performed a remarkable double-take as the cogs whirred and ground into each other. 'Mind you, my son's a journalist. When he talks to me, I have to say to him: "Son, are you talking to me as a journalist or as my son?"'

The thing about JP is that his bark is worse than his bite, and lots of the people who have worked for him liked doing so and liked him. I can't say I liked him all that much, even though I could see that there was a good man underneath it all struggling to get out. The truth is that at one level he was horribly patronised by the toffs, and his achievements often went unrecognised. But at another level, he could be very sour and grumpy. He often looked as though he was chewing wasps.

Nicholas Soames, who once entertained us all hugely at a *Tribune* dinner at the Gay Hussar, used to shout across the floor of the House, 'G and T, Giovanni!', reminding JP of his humble origins as a ship's steward. On retirement from the Commons, JP helped lead the charge on Rupert Murdoch's News Corporation over alleged phone-hacking – and those with long memories will recall how he originally made his name as a young MEP, campaigning extremely hard on behalf of patients who had become dependent on drugs produced by Roche Pharmaceuticals.

But at another level, JP was sometimes out of his depth. The late John Garrett, former MP for Norwich South, told me how as a Shadow Industry Spokesman he was asked on to respond to the news that the Pallion Shipyard on Wearside was closing down. 'Prezza demanded to see me, and told me that he – not I – would respond, and could he "have my notes"? An hour or so later and JP was back on the phone furiously demanding I return to his office – the one with portholes overlooking Big Ben. He was surrounded by screwed-up bits of paper, and started ranting and raving. The long and the short of it was that he couldn't get his head round it, so I ended up giving the speech after all.'

Garrett had always been convinced that one day JP would literally explode, like Mr Creosote in Monty Python's *Meaning of Life*.

I witnessed a JP mini-explosion myself, back in the early 1990s. I had persuaded him to come and speak at Norwich Labour Club for a *Tribune* fund-raising do. Ever the old trouper, he agreed, and seemed to be enjoying himself until it came to question time, and a train driver got up at the back and asked an anguished question about access to children for divorced fathers, such as himself. Suddenly the bold, confident JP dissolved into a panicky, skittish JP. He turned to the councillor to his right, but got no joy there. He then turned to me.

'What do I bloody well say, then?'

'I've no idea John, I'm sorry. I don't know the answer'.

A clearly irritated JP flung some verbal acrobatics in the direction of the train driver, which failed to impress, whereupon the two got into a verbal altercation.

But this was as nothing to the following week, when JP came on the phone to me. 'You promised to publish a full bloody report on that bloody meeting, and you bloody well haven't!'

'I'm sorry John. We were right out of space – but I did put something in the diary.'

At which point JP went ballistic, letting loose a stream of invective and consciousness so intense that I was utterly lost for words and decided on the method of least resistance: i.e. not responding at all. This seemed to work, as eventually the flow slowed and quietened and ended with what might be compared to some verbal 'pop-popping'. Finally JP concluded, 'Well, that's it then.' I was left in shock.

You have to agree that John Garrett had had a point about JP one day self-detonating. Although he is still blustering and fulminating as strongly as ever, he remains an unexploded device, still waiting to go off. I hope he well and truly explodes somewhere near Rupert Murdoch – that would finally teach the 'Dirty Digger' to mess with John Prescott.

All the same, I wouldn't miss JP all that much, I thought as I shuffled away my NEC papers for the last time.

Taking the Emir's Riyal –
the Al Jazeera years

I MET STEVE Clark, the first Director of News for Al Jazeera International, later to become Al Jazeera English, when he was still working for Sky TV, producing the 'Littlejohn Show'. He and Jo Burgin would get me in from time to time to argue the toss about whatever Richard Littlejohn had decided was the story of the day. Quite why the powers that be at Sky TV decided to axe Littlejohn's show, I have no idea. Like his politics or loathe them, Littlejohn was a consummate performer. He could also be a dangerous after-show drinking partner. I only dimly recall sleeping it off one night in my old Jag in the underground car park at Associated Newspapers in Kensington.

Be that as it may, Steve Clark had worked hard to burnish the Littlejohn experience, and I immediately liked him, not least because he was a fount of stories. Steve had been a boy soldier, conscripted into the Rhodesian army at the age of sixteen, and as such had many hair-raising accounts of 'hot pursuit' into the bush after the forces of Zapu and Zanu back in the 1970s. As a sharp shooter, he had once been despatched to Lusaka in neighbouring Zambia by the Smith regime to try and bump off the late Nationalist leader, Joshua Nkomo. Nkomo was a big man, who famously got dressed as a woman on another occasion to flee Ian Smith's police across the border into Botswana. But fortunately for Joshua Nkomo – and for what was to become Zimbabwe – sharp-shooting Steve was called off at the last moment. Not that any of this had ever damaged Steve's relations with the African majority governments that followed in the wake of the final collapse of Ian Smith's UDI. In fact, through Steve and for a while, Al Jazeera became the only international television network to have a bureau in Harare.

I bumped into Steve one day when I was heading into the BBC in Millbank. I hadn't heard about the decision to axe the Littlejohn Show, but Steve didn't look too crestfallen as he told me the news. I asked him what he was up to. 'I'm setting the London Broadcast Centre for Al Jazeera TV – well, the planned English Channel that is.' I mulled it over, and then a couple of days later dropped Steve a line, and asked him if he would meet for lunch in the Gay Hussar. Steve had been in TV news and programming for most of his career, and if he was involved in a project like this, it must have serious backing. After we met for lunch, I dropped Steve another line saying that if the new channel needed a correspondent at the United Nations, would he consider me? I figured that a new international channel would bound to want someone based in New York to cover the United Nations, and having spent some time over the years getting to know various people over at UN headquarters, I thought it at least worth a try. I seem to remember adding that most of the Americans I knew seemed to like English accents. Over the years I had been a talking head, commentator and newspaper reviewer for the BBC and Sky TV. *Newsnight* had also given me fair wind to turn 'first person' packages, and I had long wanted to get to do more documentary and on-air reporting. The trouble was – and is – that in Britain you are largely judged on 'what you are' and 'what you have been'. In America, as I was to discover, it is 'what you are' and 'what you can or want to be'. In Britain, my history on the Labour left and *Tribune*, largely pigeon-holed me, although sucking up to the political class or coming from the Right didn't seem to do others much harm. Al Jazeera, on the other hand, might offer a way out of this very stereotypical British typecasting problem.

The nascent Al Jazeera operation was being run out of an office in Camden, north London. On the day I went to meet Steve Clark there in the early summer of 2005, I noticed that this planned global satellite TV station could muster about five staff, a few tables, word processors and chairs, and the rest of the expanse of office was utterly empty. There was also the beginning of an operation in Doha, Qatar, which was home to Al Jazeera Arabic, the station that was in the process of revolutionising media throughout the Arab World. The channel was financed by the Emir of Qatar, and was something of a double edged sword. On the one hand Al Jazeera put Qatar on the map. I remember being asked by someone, 'Where is Qatar in Al Jazeera?' Al Jazeera Arabic was widely seen as being unbiddable and the best and most honest source of news through much of North Africa and the Middle East, and as such had left the old wooden, state-sponsored channels desperately wanting.

Qatar was at the same time the headquarters of US Central Command, which meant that there was only so much pressure the United States could put upon one of its most dependable allies in the region. But Al Jazeera did make the Emir of Qatar incredibly unpopular in some quarters – most notably in neighbouring

Saudi Arabia. The Saudis for their part set up their own channel to counter the influence of Al Jazeera, although by the time of the Egyptian revolution, that channel, al Arabiya was looking increasingly hackneyed and irrelevant, blaming constant 'technical problems' for its reluctance to report on the events unfolding on the Arab street. With Al Jazeera English TV, the Emir had another objective: to show Americans in particular that the Middle East wasn't all about hostage-taking, Al Qaeda and women in burkhas. Al Jazeera English TV was going to be a very Arabic 'World Service'. As with the original Arabic service, a number of Brits would be recruited to get the operation under way. Later, as the network grew, there would be less need for them.

'I want you to be our UN Correspondent,' said Steve Clark, 'based in New York.' And so followed a seemingly endless three months when nothing happened, when no contract arrived, despite its always being 'in the post'. I was beginning to wonder if it ever would, when in August it finally did. It offered a good salary, a housing and schooling allowance as well as a clothing and car allowance. 'Get in touch with us', said the legal company handling the move 'when you have chosen your dream apartment!' After over a decade at the proverbial coal face at *Tribune*, it surely couldn't come better than this!

Since the Gay Hussar restaurant had effectively been my other home for the past decade, I had to have a farewell party there, with the last rites to my political and journalistic life in Britain being read by Martin Rowson and Jon Wrobel, the restaurant's manager. At this point I gifted to Wrobel a framed photograph of Arthur Scargill in full flight at a meeting in County Durham some years back – with, to his left on the stage, a young man grinning widely. The young man in question was Tony Blair. This photograph, for me, was very much like the cutting from *The Times* newspaper in

George Orwell's *Nineteen Eighty-Four*, which Winston Smith has to confine to the memory hole, thus altering history for ever. Nick Brown, Labour's avuncular Chief Whip, turned up, as did most of *Tribune* past and present. So did Michael Foot and Tony Benn, who for once were quite civil to one another.

My first assignment for 'Al Jazeera International', the channel with a name but little else, was to head off to North Korea for the annual Ariyang Mass Games. The objective was not so much the material I could bring back, but Steve Clark's hope that Al Jazeera English could be the first network to have a bureau in Pyongyang. Steve and I even headed over to the North Korean Embassy in Gunnersbury Avenue, Ealing to get the ball rolling, we hoped, with the Ambassador.

As it happened Al Jazeera got the first footage of Pyongyang's first private market, and some even more interesting footage of UN food aid being illegally sold there. Our camerawoman had managed to grab that footage while I was busy entertaining some dumbstruck North Koreans trying on a Mao era suit. The channel also got the first footage ever shot on a desperately slow journey by rail through the country up to the Chinese border. What it didn't get was the tense stand-off as we reached the border, when guards came and turned the compartment upside down. What can have gone through their heads as they came across all of the paraphernalia of a film crew? The senior border guard looked genuinely shocked. Presumably he had been told to look out for Western spies, but to find a pair of them surrounded by some of the most advanced camera technology ever seen in North Korea must have been something else. But then, the Korean man who had been sitting quietly in the carriage with us suddenly spoke. He produced a copy of the Communist daily which had a picture of our 'delegation' standing outside the birthplace of Kim Il Sung. As quickly as they had arrived, the border guards disappeared.

But little was I to know then that the launch of the channel was at least a year away. Even so, some of the footage from that epic train journey and much else from inside North Korea was re-edited and turned around into a package for broadcast within a few days of Al Jazeera International launching.

'Al Jazeera? Good luck!'

'WHEN YOU GET to Homeland Security, they will see you have an "I Visa" and will want to know who you are working for,' Steve Clark had told me. I had been slightly nervous about arriving in New York for the first time as an Al Jazeera reporter – especially because barely eighteen months earlier I had had a bad experience at JFK, when my battered old suitcase had set various alarms going and I had been ushered into offices by uniformed security men and questioned about my suitcase and my whereabouts before arriving. This had begun to seem like a bad dream. Was I about to be arrested, because apparently the suitcase was testing positive for something or other? Had it been interfered with? Had someone planted something? All of these thoughts had run through my mind, until one of the security men barked, 'How did you get here?'

'In a cab,' I said.

'Where was your bag?'

'In the trunk.'

'Was there anything else in the trunk?'

I could barely remember what if anything had been inside the back of a New York cab with my suitcase, and then I remembered it was full of plastic bags.

'Well, just some plastic bags,' I said wanly.

Suddenly a light went on, and all was sweetness and light. The plastic had rubbed against the case, producing a similar effect to plastic explosive being rubbed against my suitcase. Afterwards I reflected that the 'Birmingham Six' had never been so lucky. The plastic cards they had been playing with had left on their hands a residue similar to plastic explosive, and the rest of course is a rather dismal piece of history – one that was finally unpicked by, amongst others, former *Tribune* editor and later MP, Chris Mullin.

But there was also the small matter of being seen to be part of Al Jazeera, at a time when the Bush administration was still in its pomp and when Al Jazeera Arabic TV was widely regarded in America as a 'terrorist channel' which carried tape recordings allegedly from Osama Bin Laden and which was also accused – quite erroneously – of broadcasting beheadings of Western hostages.

'So who d'ya woik for?', enquired the burly guy inspecting my passport with 'journalist' stamped all over it in the form of an 'I Visa'. Shit! Nothing else for it, I guess, I thought. I had decided to wear a suit just for good measure. Could anyone suspect an Englishman in a suit to be a terrorist? Bonkers maybe, but terrorist? Surely not.

'Al Jazeera TV', I said. He looked at me quizzically. 'Wow, good luck!' And that was it. The stamp went into the passport and I was through.

Given that I was going to be based at the United Nations, I had asked my friend the journalist Andrew Neil where I should look for an apartment. It had to be big enough to accommodate the rest of the family who would be moving over, and also fairly central.

Andrew suggested Midtown, and sent over the rental section of the *New York Times*. Within a couple of weeks of settling into a block between Second and Third Avenues with a panoramic view uptown of the Manhattan skyline, I was invited to Andrew's apartment somewhere near the top of the Trump Tower for a dinner party.

All was going swimmingly until I asked the woman I was sitting next to her name. She looked at me in bewilderment. 'Candace Bushnell!' she said abruptly.

I ploughed on. 'What do you do?'

She almost spat back, 'I'm an author! Heard of *Sex in the City*? No wonder we women don't need men anymore!'

I later discovered that part of her fury was linked to a similar conversation that she had just had with another of Andrew's guests, Emmeline Kuhn.

But sat around that table that night were others who were to become firm friends, Jennifer Jessup, Emmeline Khan, and Chantal Ribeiro – as well as others such as Ann Robinson. Andrew had introduced me to Ann before the meal started, and she had immediately concluded publicly that because I had left *Tribune* and moved to New York I must in some way have sold out: 'They all do, dear. I shouldn't worry about it.' My protestations went ignored.

Will Stebbins, Al Jazeera's Washington bureau chief, and Kieran Baker, his news editor, called up and welcomed me both to New York and to Al Jazeera. 'Where is our bureau office?', I lamely enquired. 'We don't have one yet. You are the first to arrive, so your priority is to get accredited at the UN and sort your Social Security card out.' They did tell me that they had a producer/reporter in mind to work with me in the New York start-up, and that I should call her. If I liked her, it would be very much a done deal and the pair of us could get started.

I met Kristen Saloomey over on the Upper East Side and we immediately hit it off. She had the talent and looks that Al Jazeera would be going for. Later we would be joined by an Australian cameraman Nick Castellaro and subsequently an American-Iranian producer, Melorine Mokri. We decided to call ourselves the 'Coalition of the Willing', and I went to the UN shop and bought mini US, Australian and British flags – the Iranian one would have to come later. Over the next few weeks though, the reality of my slightly parlous situation rapidly became apparent. Not only did Al Jazeera not have an office, I didn't even have a laptop. For the first few weeks in New York, I effectively ran the Al Jazeera bureau from an internet cafe on Twenty-Third street, a few blocks down from where I lived. Getting a press pass for the UN and for the New York Press Center was easier, although even to an untrained eye like mine, it seemed that the most basic of building blocks weren't in shape for the launch of a major international channel which we were repeatedly told was literally months away. The same delays began to affect my pay cheques, which for some mysterious reason stopped arriving from the December and only resumed a couple of months later. At this rate, I thought, I would be broke, jobless and in New York.

I took the Acela Express from Pennsylvania Station with Kristen to go down to Washington DC and meet Stebbins and Baker. I had told friends that our America Bureau was based in 'K Street' in Washington DC and for some reason they had all seemed quite impressed. This apparently was because K Street is home to some of the big power brokers on Capitol Hill, and to have an address there is the mark of an organisation with both power and money. We were greeted at the door by a huge African American, revolver in holster, who sent us up to the seventh floor – and building chaos. Will Stebbins gave us a guided tour of the dangling wires and half built dividing walls. 'This will be where the edit suites are situated,' he said, not altogether convincingly. Will was an old pro and an Associated Press veteran, and he also had the distinct advantage of knowing Cuba and Latin America well. When Al Jazeera finally did make it to air, the channel was by common agreement streets ahead of its competitors, both in terms of getting access to countries such as Cuba – and Venezuela, where we had a bureau – and in the scope of reporting from a part of the world with which most of the English-speaking channels rarely bothered.

I wondered why the decision had been take to locate the Al Jazeera headquarters in DC, especially since we weren't going to be concentrating coverage within the Beltway. It transpired that Al Jazeera Arabic TV had its base there and there were floors available elsewhere in the building. Be that as it may, Washington DC was a strangely antiseptic sort of town, languidly hot in the summer and bitterly cold in the winter. It was also largely empty at weekends, which is why when I was sent there to cover stories from the White House and elsewhere, I used to head out to Georgetown where there was some life and partying to be had.

In order to keep busy I would file daily reports on what was going on at the UN to Washington, presumably for Will and Kieran to read. I would get along to the noon briefings and watch Steph Dujarric, the Secretary General Kofi Annan's spokesman, being perpetually harassed by a troika of journalists from the *Times*, *Financial Times* and an obscure New York newspaper that has since folded. At the time, the oil for food scandal, which had threatened to inundate Kofi Annan, was in its final rumbles and there was a near obsessive inquisition each day at the noon briefing on the whereabouts of a Mercedes car that Annan's son apparently shouldn't have got his hands on. I used to feel sorry for Steph as he was so obviously transparently honest, and the UN Spokesman office was populated by people who gave every impression of being genuine media officers, as opposed to the deceitful political spinners back home. The trouble was that few of the rest of us journos got much of a look in, and the UN seemed incapable of wrestling the agenda back to where it wanted it to be. It also seemed bizarre that two or three print journos should effectively dominate both the agenda, and the attention of the UN Secretariat, when clearly broadcasters carried so much more potential influence.

Various other wheezes were dreamed up by Will Stebbins and others to keep us all busy, including a hostile environment course in Virginia, about twenty or miles outside DC. The DC office was beginning to fill up with all nationalities (though I was still the only Brit that had been brought over), and we trundled through the countryside and up a long dirt track, until we saw an old Confederate flag fluttering over a farmstead. A group of bearded heavies who looked as though they played for ZZ Top in their spare time stood next to a bunch of Hummers and other vehicles so vast they blocked out the sun. One of four-by-fours had a steel scrotum hanging from its fender. These guys, along with a couple of ex-SAS men and another South African former soldier who had seen military action in Namibia, were our trainers.

One of the highlights was being given the chance to fire away to our hearts' content on a succession of weaponry from revolvers to AK47s, lessons being given by 'Cleetus', who had been a firearms instructor for the military in Washington. I asked one of his friends how Cleetus had come to have a scar just above his nose. 'Yeah, well, that's where he had a Swastika tattoo. He had to have it taken off when he got his job in DC.' This rather alarming news jolted me into a new reality. Some of the young members of the new Al Jazeera team in Washington were now busy taking pictures of one another firing off various assault rifle and machine guns.

'Do you think this is a smart thing to allow?', I asked one of the ex-SAS guys whom I had begun to befriend after he admired my Ugg boots. 'Imagine one of those photos surfacing somewhere and the headline, 'Al Jazeera Terrorists On Rampage In Virginia'. He took my point, and the film was speedily erased and disposed of. A major diplomatic incident was avoided. Or should I say a major potential disaster was avoided.

Yet another wheeze to keep us busy before the launch was to send Kristen and me off to Port au Prince to film a couple of packages loosely built around the UN peace-keeping mission. I now realise just how cushy we had it back in those early days, for not only was Al Jazeera flush with cash, there was no pressure on time. We weren't on air, and this was a week or so exercise in clambering aboard UN military vehicles, blue helmets on and into the shanties of the huge, reeking slum that is the capital of Haiti. I soon realised why all of the better houses and hotels were built on the hillsides – the shit flows downwards, and most visibly could be seen in a huge brown circular smudge of sewage stretching out in the bay below. On one occasion we got onto the armoured vehicles just before the shooting started. Apparently the commander of the new Brazilian UN peacekeepers had thought it a nice idea to hand out some television sets so that a few Haitians at least got to watch the World Cup. The shooting was over the TV sets.

One afternoon outside the Presidential Palace, Kristen and the camera guy went off to get some extra film, leaving me behind in the pick-up. Out of the corner of my eye, I noticed a thin, old man sitting on top of a low wall. As he saw me look at him, he held out his hand. Why would I miss a few grubby gourds, I thought, as I plunged my hand into my pocket? The old man lumbered up to the car, but just as he took the notes from my hand, suddenly more men appeared from nowhere and then yet more. Within seconds the car was surrounded and they began to rock the vehicle. I began to get alarmed. Kris and the cameraman were oblivious to my plight, even though I could see them. If I began shouting that would show that I was really spooked. Best, I thought, to try and keep as calm as possible. Suddenly one of the men began drawing his finger across his throat, and then they all followed. 'This is it!', I thought, 'My time is up!' But just then our fixer appeared. He looked unnerved as well. But he managed to disperse the crowd with a few more grubby notes. 'I told you', he said, 'Never give money to anyone. They are so poor, everyone will come!'

'But they weren't just after money', I said, 'They were going to cut my throat!'

'No, in Haiti, when someone runs his finger across his neck, it means he's hungry ...'

Well, that was a relief, then.

Port au Prince was largely sectioned out between rival brutish gangs, and to get access to what is, and was, the poorest part of the poorest city of the poorest country in the Western hemisphere, meant having to pay homage of sorts to one of the young, wide boy gangsters who professed to love Johnnie Walker whisky and fast bikes. Having sat at his porch listening to his endless boasting, Kris the cameraman and I seemed to be accepted, and so we made our procession through Citi Soleil, a filthy huddle of corrugated hut misery, that should be burned into the mind of every visitor. The poor, benighted residents knew what they had to do, as they shook the hands of the gangster and his assorted goons.

When we got back, we didn't have the equipment to cut the piece in New York, so Kris and I went to DC and into the hands of Sol Levine, a veteran CNN producer and living proof – along with Al Jazeera's heavyweight first anchor, Dave Marash – that it was more than possible to be American and Jewish and land a job with Al Jazeera. Sol was a small man with a big heart, who liked to sound tough. His traditional greeting, when he saw me was, 'Hell, no, a bloody Brit! March into the sea, Redcoat!' But Sol was also very good at his job, and deserves credit for flying into Doha with the rest of us, and when challenged at immigration announcing his name so loudly most of the airport could hear him.

Some of my new-found American friends would advise me to 'go quiet about the Al Jazeera thing'. When I announced that I had signed up to a speakers' agency and was being sent on a tour of redneck states, it was quietly suggested that I was quite mad and would wind up dead. In fact, and on a tour that turned into an elongated eighteen-month occasional speaking hop across the Mid West, and into states further away such as Utah and Oklahoma, I never found such receptive audiences. At South Utah University for instance, over a thousand students, most of them Mormons, turned out to listen politely and ask the sort of intelligent questions that would never occur to some of our grungy crowd of non-committal students. Many of the US students had taken part in service overseas, or were engaged in charity work in developing countries. Not to be defeated by the notorious absence of a national media and endless TV and radio stations full of pap, I soon discovered that Young America was active and online, whether in Indiana or Michigan.

In Oklahoma I found myself sitting next to the chief of a local Native American tribe. He split his time between looking after the interests of his people on the reservation and coming to lecture the students I was supposed to be lecturing. I wish I could say that his name was 'Sitting Bull', but in truth I never wrote it down, and now he is just a memory. After lunch though, he summoned a people-carrier and took us off to the casino on the Indian reservation. It was of course full of white elderly Americans filling slot machines.

But the 'Al Jazeera thing' was a surefire show-opener, and being fresh off the boat, I was the toast of many a Manhattan bar and party. One of the more memorable was a drinks thrash organised by the British Mission to the United Nations. Being amongst quite a few Brits reminded me of just how stiff we can be. I had already got used to American friends telling me their life histories and innermost secrets within an hour or so of getting to know them. There was something very straightforward about most of the Americans I had met, and within a very short period any remaining prejudices I had harboured over the years had dissipated. But here I was with Ian Williams, who had got me in to the cocktail party, and advancing through the door was the somewhat retro, short-ish figure of America's Ambassador to the United Nations, whose face and moustache I had already got used to seeing pop up at press calls. 'Meet my friend Mark Seddon', said Ian to Ambassador John Bolton – for it was he. Bolton moved to shake my hand. 'He's the new UN correspondent for Al Jazeera'. Bolton, notorious neo-con that he was, did not falter, although I would like to think that his eyebrows arched and his moustache bristled. 'Welcome to America', he said.

But that welcome did not just trip off the lips of John Bolton, however insincere it may have been. Kristen and I decided that we would have to get down to the headquarters of the New York Police Department to get our press passes, which meant going with our cameraman Nick as well. It was a blistering hot, humid day, and for some reason the cab driver wouldn't put his air-conditioning on. He insisted that we roll our windows down, but still the car was getting hotter and hotter, and the sweat was rolling down my neck. 'What the hell is going on?', demanded Nick. 'I can't turn my heater off!', whimpered the driver.

In truth I was just a little nervous about visiting the NYPD. We were Al Jazeera after all. But once inside, all went with brisk efficiency. Then a cop barked, 'Deputy Commissioner Ray Kelly wants to see you!' This is it, I thought. Something bad is going to happen.

In fact nothing worse happened than a cup of coffee and a private introduction to the NYPD, what it did, and background on the huge number of linguistic groups that made up the force. And all courtesy of a very senior, busy senior police officer, who was the epitome of courtesy itself. Ray Kelly is today Chief Commissioner of the NYPD, and I was glad to have made his acquaintance. Then he was Deputy Commissioner. The idea that the Deputy Commissioner of the Metropolitan Police in London might invite foreign journalists in for coffee and a chat is of course too fanciful to imagine.

On the celebs

MANHATTAN IS OF course the place for spotting celebs. Unlike my good friend, Martin Rowson, I haven't been much of a star-fucker in my time, but if I think about it I did have one or two brushes with celebrity in New York. Since celebrity apparently shifts books, I may as well make mention of a few of them here.

One baking hot August day, I was heading back to my apartment above Central Park on Madison Avenue, when a fast moving posse almost pushed me off the sidewalk. The tallest of the dark-suited, dark-glasses wearing men was none other than Arnie Schwarzenegger, who some years earlier Californians in a collective fit of madness had made their State Governor. 'Hey, Arnie!', shouted a cab driver, 'Where yer headin?' Since it was transparently obvious that Arnie and his crew were heading in a straight line up Madison Avenue, I couldn't work out why the cabbie had bothered.

On another occasion I was sitting with Andrew Neil and a few of his friends who happened to be in New York, including the future editor of *The Spectator*, Fraser Nelson, when a ludicrous figure dressed as a cowboy came in and sat behind us in deep whispered conversation with an ancient man who looked as though he had just stepped out of a bad 1970s gangster movie. On close inspection, and beyond the massive dark glasses, I recognised Yoko Ono. This wasn't to be my only at-a-distance brush with people linked to the Beatles. Al Jazeera's PR man in the city was Peter Brown, with whom I used to have lunch regularly. We would also go to the same Midtown restaurant where media people such as Tina Brown would want to be spotted. Peter Brown had been manager of the Beatles, and features in one of the group's final singles, 'The Ballad of John and Yoko', where John Lennon immortalised Peter in the lines, 'Peter Brown called to say, / "You can make it OK, / You can get married in Gibraltar near Spain."'

Whether he fits neatly into the 'celebrity bracket' is a moot point, not least to President Hugo Chavez of Venezuela, who must at least see himself as some kind of celebrity back home, since his TV appearances – or monologues – can last hours. Chavez, unlike Fidel Castro in Cuba, came to power via the ballot box, and has been returned to power via the ballot box despite the increasingly Bonapartist nature of his regime. I could understand the Left's enthusiasm for him, although I didn't entirely share it. But now that he was coming to New York to speak at the UN General Assembly, perhaps there would be the chance to interview the man and find out what really made him tick. I religiously began to attend as many of the socials at the Venezuelan Mission that I could in order to ingratiate myself with the Ambassador. Promises were made, but as I was to discover a Venezuelan promise may not be all that it seems. 'Yes, Mr Seddon, Mr President likes Al Jazeera. He will be looking forward to meeting you when he arrives.' It was true that our DC Bureau Chief, Will Stebbins, had smartly decided that it would be a good idea to open the network's first South American bureau in Caracas.

Eventually the day arrived for the supposed interview. Kris, Nick and I duly turned up at the Mission, to be told that the President 'has gone to meet the people in the Bronx.' What followed was a bizarre game of cat-and-mouse as we attempted to follow the Presidential cavalcade and wound up outside a large church hall in a battered street of tenements. I was relieved to see my old friend, the left-wing academic Cornell West, with whom I had shared a number of platforms with over the years. 'Yeah, sure, he's in there.' And so he was: President Hugo Chavez in full flow to a packed congregation of the urban poor – and strangely a row of Native Americans in traditional Mohawk gear who were sitting impassively in the front. It soon transpired that we were not going to be getting the interview, but instead rather a good story. Essentially, the Venezuelans were helping to subsidise fuel oil for some of America's poor, which explained (a) why he was speaking in the Bronx and (b) why the Mohawk had shown up. By my reckoning Chavez's monologue lasted at least a couple of hours, and without notes. (The only other person I had ever seen manage this with any success was our very own Arthur Scargill.) Accompanying the President was a phalanx of extremely attractive girls, draped in red sashes. I wondered if the pouting Chavez had a female praetorian guard like the mad Muammar Gaddafi?

Soon after Al Jazeera finally launched, news arrived that George Clooney and his father would be visiting UN headquarters, as part of the ongoing campaign to try and stop the Sudanese from continuing to commit genocide in Darfur. The desk in DC came on the phone wanting to know if we could get an interview with him, which I thought highly unlikely. But Kristen clearly thought differently. She tracked down his agent and kept on pushing the request. In an act of remarkable generosity, she solemnly told the news editor in DC that 'Mark will be doing the interview.'

At the time, Kristen was a producer/reporter. Even still, had she pushed to do the interview, I wouldn't have got in her way.

Clooney's support for the Darfur campaign was hugely influential. There is nothing like the backing of a global celeb to kick-start any campaign. But Clooney – and his father – were both real gents too. They could have simply gone through the motions, and performed some do-goodery that their agents would know brings yet more kudos. George Clooney was briefed to a tee, passionate and persuasive. I interviewed him in the General Assembly building, with Kristen producing and Nick filming. As we finished I heard someone ask if we could have a group photo. I'm not sure if it still exists, but remarkably, it featured some twenty-odd souls. People – well young women – had suddenly appeared from nowhere, and were all angling to get as close to Clooney as possible.

The actress Mia Farrow was another great supporter of African causes, and following the success of the Clooney interview, I was keen to get to her too. I interviewed her a couple of times, since she had been to the Sudan and Chad and witnessed some of the brutality ritually displayed to women in particular. We appeared to hit it off, and we would talk quite regularly on the phone, although never straying from African affairs to anything vaguely personal. At the time I was lobbying the bosses in Doha to let me report on one of the longest running and most brutish wars, that which disfigured the Democratic Republic of Congo. Some four million people had died in a brutal conflict seemingly without end, with civilians, particularly women, largely at the receiving end. Mia Farrow was now intent on returning to Chad and living for a year in a typical African village in order to focus international attention on the suffering of women. Once I had told her about the situation in the Eastern Congo, she wanted to go there instead. 'You and

I should make the film, the documentary on what is happening there,' she told me one evening. I couldn't believe my luck! What an opportunity! Nick Castellaro was preparing to pack his bags. But for some reason best known to them, the bosses in Doha said 'No'.

Ban Ki-Moon and the UN

IT WAS THE best part of a year before we finally managed to get studio and office space at UN headquarters. Mark Malloch Brown – who went on to be a Foreign Office Minister under Gordon Brown, and the best of Brown's 'Goats' by far – was helpful, as was Shashi Tharoor, the charismatic public face of the UN's Department of Public Information. But it didn't help that Al Jazeera wasn't on air, and that we had no real idea when it would be.

Wandering the corridors of the UN in those early days left me with the impression of an organisation that had been under siege and was in slow decline. The building was shabby and run down, the offices inhabited by a number of the world's media strangely reminiscent of the tatty spaces which *Tribune* had inhabited over the years. Amazingly, the press corps contained people who had retired decades before but who hadn't been moved out of their old offices. For them the UN was a bit of a social club, rather like the House of Lords. The office next door to us contained an elderly lady who had a typewriter and towering, tottering, piles of yellow paper. Next door to her was an even older Austrian couple. The name of their former publication was featured on the door in the sort of Gothic writing of pre-war Prussia. They didn't even have a typewriter. One former journalist of advanced years would appear with her plastic bags and occupy a phone booth for most of the day before shuffling off to buy a coffee.

Presiding over this menagerie was a mighty fine Canadian fellow by the name of Gary Fowlie. He had the most extraordinary quality of calmness under fire, which I suppose is a major recommendation for working for the United Nations. Gary was our 'go-to man', and from time to time when the cameras are following various ambassadors at the 'stakeout' I still spot him. The task of clearing out the menagerie unhappily fell upon him.

Folklore has it that Kofi Annan was a UN Secretary General of rare charisma, although in all the press conferences I attended and speeches I listened to, there wasn't a great deal of evidence for that. But he had a certain aura of moral authority; not that this was enough to save him from the constant barbs of the Bush Administration and the Asterix-lookalike US Ambassador, the neo-con John Bolton.

The UN was terribly hobbled by US Republican hostility, so much so that there was speculation that the organisation might one day abandon Manhattan altogether and head for Geneva. The headquarters was actually built on land that had housed, amongst other things, a meat market: at least, that is what John Goelet, whose family had once owned it (and whose family once rivalled the Astors in terms of their real estate wealth) once told me.

I never really got that close to Annan. There was always a reason why he couldn't do an interview, and in any event another member of the UN press corps who had just joined Al Jazeera, Ghida Fakhry, knew him much better and filmed a documentary with him in his native Ghana to coincide with the launch of the network.

Ban Ki-Moon was a different case. The UN Press corps had of course heard that a former Korean Foreign Minister was being talked of as Annan's successor, but the charming, erudite spokesman and author Shashi Tharoor had the journalists' vote. Here was someone who had opinions, who was good on television and didn't speak in diplomatic babble. For many of us he seemed the obvious successor, and would surely get the votes from the South. As it turned out, when the white smoke did emerge it was for Ban. We, along with Laura Trevelyan of the BBC and Al Jazeera Arabic's charming Abderrahim Foukara, were the first to interview the new Secretary General designate at the South Korean Mission not far from the UN. He came across as someone who was deadly serious about the burden he was about to inherit and as a man capable of hard work on an epic scale. English was his second language and he had promised to take French lessons, but his English was halting and he was sometimes difficult to understand.

Over the next few months I got to know him quite well, not least I suspect because he preferred dealing with television journalists than print journalists. One of the latter had effectively tied Ban up in knots at his first press conference, bowling in a question about capital punishment. The SG had sounded equivocal over an issue that the UN was clear about: namely that there was no place for the death penalty.

By this time I had risen to the dizzy heights of Vice President of the UN Correspondents' Association, and so a new line of communication opened up to some of Ban's key aides, notably his Chef de Cabinet Kim Won-soo and his Director of Communications, Mike Meyer. The former had come with Ban from the Korean foreign service, while Mike was an award-winning journalist and author. Whatever the UN lacked in terms of facilities and whatever the UN often failed to be, it more than made up for with the quality of some of its key staffers.

I managed to persuade both the SG's office and my bosses in Washington and Doha that I should accompany Ban on one of his first big trips overseas, to Africa. What followed was one of those crowning periods in journalism, not just because of the stories but because of the places and people we visited and met. From Cairo we flew to Entebbe in Uganda; from Entebbe we headed out to Kinshasa, the sprawling, heaving, humid slum that is the capital of the Democratic Republic of Congo. Here Ban was to meet with the new President Joseph Kabila and with an American UN legend in William Lacy Swing, the Secretary General's Special Representative to the DRC. Swing might just as well have been called 'Governor General', for the UN force over which he presided provided much of the glue that held this ramshackle country together.

Throughout the tropics the rainforest is in retreat, but in the Congo it is fast returning, pushing up even in the streets of the capital. Wearing blue peacekeeper helmets, Nick and I headed out past the huge mouldering stadium where Muhammad Ali had famously fought his 'Rumble in the Jungle' with George Foreman in 1974. During the recent elections the UN had set up some mobile ballot stations, but all were shredded literally within minutes by the sheer mass of people who had come to vote – and to pinch the plastic for their roofs.

The following day we abandoned our regular UN plane for a smaller aircraft that was to fly us to Kisangani in the heart of the forest. One of Ban's predecessors, the much revered Dag Hammerskjold, had lost his life when his plane crashed somewhere just over the Congo's borders in what was then Northern Rhodesia. I thought of him as our plane bucked and jolted through a massive thunderstorm, whose streaks of lightning would suddenly illuminate the seemingly endless forest below. During these flights, Ban would leave his seat and wander down the plane to speak to us journalists. Courteous to a fault, the impression he left was one of quite a humble man. To me this was confirmed by someone I met who used to take in Ban's laundry. 'His shirts are worn, sometimes almost threadbare,' he confided. Ban had been old enough to witness many of the horrors of the Korean War, and in the years since had not sought riches or aggrandisement. It occurred to me then that Ban was one of those rare 'good guys' who make it to the top, and I haven't changed my mind about him since. On occasions – for instance, after Kisangani we flew to Nairobi and then Addis Ababa for the African Union summit – he would invite us journalists for lunch or dinner. Although he may have been uncomfortable speaking at large press gatherings, he seemed quite at home in small, informal groups.

Much of the Western media really couldn't get a grip on Ban Ki-Moon. For them he lacked the charisma of his predecessor Kofi Annan. I could never quite see what the excitement was all about with Annan. For a start there was nothing particularly charismatic about him, and his later years at the UN were mired in the 'Oil for Food' scandal and weakness in the face of admittedly extraordinary provocation from the Bush administration.

Ban Ki-Moon has had the advantage of working with a rather different US administration than his predecessor. He has grown in office and whatever some of his earlier detractors may have claimed, is very much his own man.

Later I was part of the press corps that went with Ban to the Middle East, which was an altogether more luxurious affair as the Emir of Qatar wouldn't accept that the Secretary General should fly around the Levant in the ageing UN plane. Instead he lent one from Qatar Airlines; or rather, he lent the most luxurious plane in the fleet. When the Syrian Foreign Minister joined us in Amman *en route* to Damascus, we were invited to film both Ban and the foreign minister in deep discussion as we flew. But somehow it seemed a bit of an impertinence to disturb us hacks who were busy sampling the best of what the Emir could offer.

When we arrived on the final leg of the visit in Doha, Nick Castellaro was selected as the pool cameraman, which was not surprising as he was the best. In any event all of his colleagues owed him big-time, for his one man set-up for all of the interviews conducted with Ban in Nairobi. 'Mate', said Nick when he got back. 'It got a bit hairy in there. While I was filming Ban arriving, I turned my back on the Emir. This big guy took me to one side and gave me a right bollocking. But then, you'll never believe this, the Emir looked over, saw the motif on my cap and said, "Don't worry, he is from Al Jazeera."'

New York! New York!

IT IS ONE thing to go to New York for a weekend or a short holiday, quite another to live in this most extraordinary city. Appearances deceive and New York is of course an old city; old in the sense that the Empire State Building has ancient elevators, that many buildings are heated by even more ancient heating systems, and that in comparison to Beijing, Taipei or Shanghai, New York is, well, just a little dilapidated. It used to be even more dilapidated, crime-ridden and grubby, but the city underwent something of a renaissance from the 1980s onwards – even if it left much of its edgy personality behind with it.

Most of even older New York disappeared a long time ago, but I took special delight in discovering English elm trees, planted by British settlers in some of the Manhattan Parks. The most famous was, and is, 'Hangman's Elm' in Washington Square, which had reportedly been used as a gibbet – although others claim that the tree was planted overlooking a burial ground for the executed of New York City. I would take great delight occasionally, being so far from home and on my own, to wander down to this tree and tell passing New Yorkers its history. For it had been planted as a line of elms to mark the boundary of the long-since-disappeared Herring Farm. They must have thought me mad, but then the real glory of New York is the refreshing ability of city dwellers either to ignore or simply tolerate generalised madness, which is frankly, all around.

Take for instance the man whom I often saw dressed as the incredible hulk wandering along Third Avenue, who had even painted his dog green. Or there was the black guy in a white three-piece suit and matching bowler hat whom I would frequently meet at the local check-out. The point is that no one ever batted an eyelid, however outlandish anyone was dressed.

The glorious thing about New York is of course the infinite capacity of New Yorkers to reinvent themselves. As I said earlier of the wider USA, as a rule of thumb in New York you are largely defined by what you are and who you want to be. In Britain you can be typecast and frozen in a place, unable ever truly to escape. In New York, transience and fashion rule supreme. I never found it easier anywhere else to get into parties as I did in that city. There was always something going on, and it didn't seem to matter that one evening it could be a room full of artists or the next a bunch of hedge fund managers.

The transience was scary, though. Each year thousands of America's smartest and most attractive girls graduate and try and make it in New York, as do hordes of young men. Rents are higher now than during the glory days of punk and disco, the days of the Ramones and the New York Dolls, and so the kids have less time to prove themselves. It's tough, sometimes verging on the feral. Sometimes I would think that it would be so easy just to disappear, fall under the radar and for no one to notice or even care. Here, despite the fact that this was the city that never slept and in which anything and everything was possible – and available – older, less progressive mating habits persisted. A good number of the best looking women would try and make out with the new nobility, the bankers and the hedge funders. Most of that particular breed never failed to disappoint with their crass, ignorant conservative ways. But for the girls here was money and the good time, even if it meant having to act like a gangster's moll.

The flip side in New York – I should say even in New York, which has the highest union membership of any American city – is the hire, fire and leave overnight culture. Since Al Jazeera was registered with Ofcom in London, our vacation and employment agreements tended to mirror those of Britain. Americans were staggered to learn that employees had the right to hand in their notice and work through it. In the US you could be in a job one day and out of it the next. The biggest bugbear though was the country's creaking healthcare system, that notoriously failed to cover over 40 million citizens and was a benchmark for ludicrous amounts of paper shuffling and wastage, even if, for the well insured, some of New York's hospitals were amongst the best in the world.

My own brief contact with the crazy world of American health insurance occurred after my daughter had slipped near our apartment in Kipps Bay and hurt her arm. Despite the fact that I had company health insurance with a health insurance provider, I was soon deluged with letters and forms to fill in. It transpired that despite the fact that I was paying health insurance, I still owed the hospital, or some company linked to the hospital $350. The letters and forms must have cost at least that amount.

Another myth soon to be exploded was the idea that somehow I had left a country that was hidebound by high taxes, an engorged public sector and an inefficient welfare state. I was staggered to see the tax hit from my first salary packet. Not only was I paying

Federal Tax, I had to pay New York State Tax and then New York City Tax. On top of that I paid for social security. In fact I was paying as a proportion a higher rate of tax that I would have been in Britain – and that didn't include the heavy hitter of a tax, health insurance, which was fortunately paid for by the company. I used to enjoy winding Andrew Neil up about New York's apology for an enterprise culture.

As the cold weather approached, I was staggered to see people emerge with their toy pet dogs dressed in little coats and hats and made-to-measure boots. New York is a city of singletons, and as my friend and Al Jazeera Arabic cameraman Glenn would say, 'Weird, New York shut in people.' Some of these good burghers lived for their dogs or cats, some of whom would rarely emerge at all from apartments, growing corpulent in the process. Come early Sunday morning though, when I was sometimes called into the studio to do a live piece, I would come across hordes of dog owners, all pooping the scoop as tonnes of excrement was laid upon Manhattan's notoriously grubby sidewalks. Still, I thought, at least the owners pick it up. Now, when I've been marooned in the posher districts of Paris …

One of the security men at the Reuters building in Times Square where we had our other office was an American Irish guy called Jerry. Since he spent most of his time standing outside the building he was a fount of all knowledge with regard to what was going on in the area. One morning he asked if I wanted to go to the NYPD Memorial Concert in the Town Hall, which wasn't that far away from where we were standing, since 'Pat' – an ex-cop turned Times Square security man – would be playing the pipes. We met before it all kicked off in an Irish bar. 'Meet Ritchie,' said Jerry. 'If Ritchie don't like you, Ritchie'll waste you!' A great, grey slab of a man sat at the bar festooned in bling and wearing dark glasses.

Ritchie was here too for the concert, but I was not too anxious to ask him many questions. In any event he looked me up and down and returned to his beer. 'He's a Westie,' Jerry told me. In other words part of the old Irish mob.

What followed in the Town Hall was a New York equivalent of Last Night of the Proms, except that the patriotic fervour was even more intense. Lots of mawkish military singers and hands on hearts. It was times like this that I used to hope that no one would get around to asking me what I did for a living. It wouldn't have mattered, I don't suppose, that I gave regularly to a charity for a retired NYPD cops: Al Jazeera was Al Jazeera. Afterwards, camera in hand – I was doing a first-person report for the network – Jerry and I stumbled after the marching band of the NYPD Emerald Society as the pipes and drums went echoing down the avenues. It was a hot and humid evening, and Jerry, despite having had a few, was getting thirsty. Away the marching column went around the corner and I bumped into a girl with short blonde hair and black shorts. She was a snapper for the *New York Post*, she said, and couldn't get high enough to take a shot. I helped her stand on the fender of a parked van. 'Do you want to come to a party downtown after?' I looked over at Jerry, and thought, 'I can't just abandon him half pissed,' and so I passed on it. Instead, Jerry and I went off in search of the Irish bars that he promised me were worth having a glass or two in. Even though we were both half cut by now, we began slowly to sober up – especially Jerry. 'They've all closed down,' he said to himself sadly. Most of them had. Most of the Irish bars of Jerry's youth had long ago shut up shop, because Manhattan evolves at a speed that Londoners can only imagine.

Giorgio Gomelsky

MOST NEW YORKERS seemed to like Brits, and in any event the city's class system, although pretty elaborate, didn't appear to revolve around accent or where you came from. At the rare times that New Yorkers were thrown together, they tended to rise to the challenge. On one occasion the transit workers went on strike and the subway was shut down for two days. The union was led by an American Haitian called Roger Toussaint, named after the firebrand revolutionary who helped throw Napoleon's army out of Hispaniola. Fortunately for him, perhaps, the now non-travelling New Yorkers had no inkling at all of this historical coincidence. Mayor Bloomberg decreed that cabs for hire to be shared, and so followed one extraordinary day when I took three cabs to get from the United Nations to go and see my old friend Giorgio Gomelsky at his 'Zu Club' in the Garment District. The first cab contained three smart-looking young women trying to get to work – two white, one black. During the course of the short journey one of them told me her life story and about her shitty, no good boyfriend. She also asked me out. The next shared cab contained a couple of Jewish diamond traders, who wanted to know what I did. They seemed shocked when I told them, but thought it was hilarious that one of the first things I had done for Al Jazeera in New York was to set up the company taxi account with Tel Aviv Taxis. The last cab contained three men, including one Asian guy who was blind. He had made his first million, and was in the process of explaining how I could make mine, when fortunately Giorgio's club came into view.

I had met Giorgio well before I moved to New York, at the instigation of my old friend and former agent, Jo Philips. It had been at the launch of John Strausbaugh's epic tome on 'colostomy rockers', entitled *Rock 'Til You Drop*, which I had persuaded the *Evening Standard* to allow me to review. Strausbaugh had dedicated his hilarious and outrageous book to Giorgio, the unassuming Georgian who had played such an enormous but understated part in the music scene on both sides of the Atlantic. The book event was at Giorgio's club, which had seen the launch – and stage death – of many a singer and acts. The place was packed with the sort of eclectic crowd that only New York could produce, and outside I smoked a cigarette with a Romanian stripper who had just come off duty.

I loved Giorgio partly because he was fount of such wonderful stories and vignettes about a world I didn't know much about, but also because he was an unashamed Marxist and enthusiast for Al Jazeera. I used to get along to his club – which had apparently been a sex shop in the dim and distant past – to listen to whoever Giorgio had decided to feature. The Zu Club had always been open to new talent, and still maintained its avant-garde risqué edge, even as CBGBs was spluttering to a close. Giorgio was a film-maker, impresario, music manager, songwriter (as Oscar Rasputin) and record producer. He owned the Crawdaddy Club, where the Rolling Stones were the house band, and he was involved with their early management. That was in a London, where the idea of a good night out was to go and visit a milk bar. Despite my persistent questioning, Giorgio was always loyal to Mick Jagger – even though I had heard from others that Jagger hadn't treated Giorgio too well. Giorgio hired the Yardbirds as a replacement and managed them. He was also their producer from the beginning through 1966. In 1967 he started Marmalade Records (distributed by Polydor), which featured Julie Driscoll, Brian Auger and The Trinity, The Blossom Toes, and early recordings by Graham Gouldman, Kevin Godley and Lol Creme, who became 10cc. Giorgio was also instrumental in the careers of the Soft Machine, David Allen and Gong, and Magma.

But to run through Giorgio's illustrious career would probably take another chapter. Suffice to say that I used to look forward to getting round to seeing him in his upstairs apartment, full of state-of-the-art recording equipment. Whenever I went to New York I would take some tea or marmalade from Britain with me to give to Giorgio. I realised after a while that despite our age difference and hugely different lives, we were kindred spirits of a sort. Giorgio was a lifelong rebel, and he was an enthusiastic supporter of the early Manhattan punk scene, but it was all for a purpose. In the early days he wanted his club to be the base for the progressive European music scene to influence the rather predictable and staid American music scene. In this he had been hugely successful. This, I used to think to myself in moments of exhilaration, was what I should be doing with Al Jazeera in New York.

I also think that despite the fact that Manhattan had long been Giorgio's home, he sometimes felt stifled by the banality of some of America and hankered after London and Europe. I knew that was the case finally when he came to my New York leaving do, and told me how lucky I was to be going 'back to civilisation'.

London calling

FOR ME, LEAVING New York was one of the hardest things I have ever had to do. In just over two hugely eventful, hilarious and deeply stimulating years, I had made some lasting friends, helped create a new TV channel in a land that was supposed to be deeply hostile, and in truth put down some roots in a city I had come to love. I had lived in Midtown and on Madison Avenue; mine was the first trans-Atlantic 'live' for Al Jazeera; and I had come to know and appreciate the United Nations. I had reported from outside the White House, from Times Square and from the gaping maw that was where the Twin Towers had once stood. I had travelled on speaking tours from Halifax, Nova Scotia, to Hancock, Michigan; to Las Vegas and to Boston; the Catskills and Vermont; Woodstock and the Andes. My apartment in Kipps Bay looked uptown to the United Nations, and over to the beautifully lit Times Square. These places and the friends who lived there had become my second home. And nothing would ever let me miss the vivid, vibrant colours of the American fall. I would have stayed in America, of course, had my family not already returned to Britain a year earlier.

Returning to London felt like a defeat. I had promised myself that I wouldn't be coming back. I had opted to stay with Al Jazeera, despite the fact that there seemed to be some confusion as to what I would be doing in London, and despite the fact that I had been offered another job in PR. My news editor Steve Clark told me that that I would be spending most of my time in Europe, but that given my connections to the UN, I would be returning to report from New York from time to time. The letter of agreement said that I would be the network's 'Diplomatic Correspondent', which cheered me up, as I always felt that I was a stronger as a talking head, giving analysis, rather than as a reporter turning packages. It soon transpired, however, that whatever promises had been made or written down did not count for very much. I was asked by the London news editor not to describe myself as the Diplomatic Correspondent, and soon settled into a role of turning up to Al Jazeera's basement broadcast centre in London in order to report news of the day. And since the network unsurprisingly weren't much interested in bog-standard UK news of the day stories, and since there were already a number of reporters who had been based in London from the beginning, I soon began to feel semi-redundant and unchallenged. I realised that the game was up when one evening I got a call from someone who wasn't even attached to the planning desk. Al Jazeera could be horribly disorganised, and this had the feeling of a disaster waiting to happen. 'Can you get down to the LSE tomorrow for a 9am live?', came the request. 'What's the story?', I asked. 'Something to do with the Gurkhas, apparently.'

The car was late and the traffic on the M1 into London abysmal. I had looked up 'LSE and Gurkhas', and found that there was a statue of a Gurkha near the London School of Economics. I presumed that I would be bowled a few questions on the continuing legal case, so I called the desk to ask for a lead on the questions. 'London School of Economics! What the fuck are you doing there? You're supposed to be at the London Stock Exchange. The financial markets are in free fall – or didn't you know?'

As a reporter one is supposed to be able to turn a hand to whatever the story, whichever the place. I had gone from print to television and learned the trade. I had been sent to Spain to cover an oil conference and ended up reporting a football match, just as I had had to turn seemingly endless agency packages about obscure skirmishes in eastern Turkey. But financial news was something I knew nothing about.

In Wall Street reporters still have traders hollering as a backdrop behind them. In the London Stock Exchange there are a series of small studios to rent, with screens inside that have graphs denoting what the NASDAQ or the Dow is doing, none of which made any sense whatsoever to me. My 'live', as the global economy tanked, was to be in ten minutes for Doha. What the hell was I supposed to do? I reached out and grabbed some newspapers. As the credits rolled, I kicked off proceedings with a newspaper review of sorts on the state of the markets.

I thought I had handled what was a difficult situation reasonably well. The Director of News, Al Anstey, did not. I ended up having a running row with him as we attempted to do some follow up interviews in a central London market. I realised then that there would be no real attempt to give me the role I had been promised, and that the chaos of Al Jazeera, hugely stimulating once, had now completely worn me down. What was depressing was the number of round pegs in square holes that the network had managed to create – and in such a short time. Reporters on other networks would often say how much they envied people like me working for Al Jazeera, and in the early days they certainly did have a lot to envy. What they didn't appreciate, however, was that typically a reporter for our network would be in position first and leave last. While others reported and packaged for one broadcast centre, we would often be doing it for four broadcast centres around the globe. I lost count of the times when I would be in position for, say, Kuala Lumpur at 7.00am, then it would move to Doha, then London and finally to Washington DC with an 'as live'. It would often be midnight before we were packing our gear. Since the news desk staff would change with each broadcast centre, there was usually no one to look after our interests, and those of the crew on the ground. Sometimes the demands became overwhelming.

But then Al Jazeera is the closest thing to an ongoing revolution, the sort that Chou En Lai would have recognised. Five years since its launch, it has been difficult to find many familiar faces, especially at managerial level. But what Al Jazeera has more than made up for is the public perception, right across the globe, that it is a serious TV channel, and relatively unbiased. It came into its own following Israel's invasion of Gaza and was doing so again in 2011 as the Arab Spring changed the face of the Middle East. Even without the much needed investment in PR and distribution in North America that so many of us always wanted to see, Al Jazeera is making real strides amongst the young web-media generation. So whenever the channel came under attack, I could never kill the habit of coming to its defence. In August 2011, Al Jazeera finally announced that it was launching – on television – in New York City. My old news editor Kieran Baker had sent me the press release, which I read with a mixture of real delight and some sadness that I wasn't there to see it.

In search of heroes: Lech Walesa

WHAT HAPPENS WHEN a teenage hero turns out to be something of, well, a disappointment? More to the point, what happens when an internationally recognised Nobel Peace Prize winner, who played a pivotal role in the downfall of Communism, turns out to be strangely incoherent? Back in the early 1980s, I wore a Solidarnosc – or Solidarity – badge with pride, and was once stopped by customs officers at Dover and questioned as to my nationality as I was wearing it. Years later, Keith Vaz MP invited me to one of his myriad awards dinners in Parliament, at which Walesa was a guest. I was a little bit wary, as the previous awards dinner that Keith had invited me to had been for the President of Malta, during which Keith had announced, 'And now may I ask Mark Seddon to make the loyal toast to her Majesty the Queen!' After this embarrassment, and being asked to give a present to Lech Walesa, I wondered if I might be required to deliver a loyal toast again.

Still later, and now back with Al Jazeera TV in London, I had pitched three stories that I knew would take me to Poland for a week. The first was the growing conflict between Polish environmentalists and the coal industry, which I knew would entail a trip down a Silesian coal mine.

The second was the controversial decision of the US to station a base for its Strategic Defence Shield on an old Warsaw Pact base in Pomerania, during which our crew ended up dining at one of Adolf Hitler and Eva Braun's favourite hotels in Zopot, in what had once been part of East Prussia not far from Gdansk. There – in the dying days of the Second World War, we were told, the fanatical Gauleiter of Konigsberg, Erich Koch, had refused to allow the civilian population to flee as the Red Army wrought its terrible revenge for the millions killed by the Nazis. Eventually tens of thousands escaped the burning inferno that was Konigsberg and headed across the ice before it began to crack under heavy bombardment. They fell headlong in with horses, carts and whatever they had managed to salvage.

This part of the Baltic coast is justly famed for the amber that is washed up along the beaches and long Spits. But the sea sometimes disgorges something that is rarely referred too. During stormy weather the lagoon that stretched out beyond where we were sitting would still occasionally release a deadly flotsam of human and animal bones that would wash up on the beach. Konigsberg remains today the isolated Russian enclave of Kaliningrad, one of the few Soviet era cities to retain the name of a leading Bolshevik.

Much of Pomerania and Silesia passed to Poland, but here memories are long and bitter. As our crew was decamping into the old German-era Rathaus, or town hall, in Slupsk to interview the Mayor, an elderly lady started shouting at us. 'Raus! Raus!', she bellowed. 'I thought all of the Germans were long gone from round here,' I said to Chris, our Polish translator. 'Yes, they are – that woman was Polish. It's just that she thinks any foreigners must be Germans and her generation still hates them with a vengeance.' Once in the Mayor's office, we met another elderly woman, who was introduced as 'our town's friend from Munich'. She told us that she had been born in Slupsk, or 'Stolp' as it had been known, and had been forced to march west with the rest of the German population from the eastern territories. With the fall of Communism came her chance, and now she was doing her bit to try and heal the divide, having recently unveiled a statue – for which she had helped raise funds – to the town's Jews who had been murdered by the Nazis.

We had travelled to Slupsk from Gdansk by car, a journey so hair-raising and dangerous that I genuinely thought we were destined to have a terrible accident that night. The Polish road network may have benefited from some EU largesse, but this part of northern Poland didn't appear to have seen much of it. Not only were the roads appalling, they were covered in snow and ice. Visibility was abysmal, as we slipped and slid our way across the wintry countryside.

The third story was around the imminent threat of closure facing three Polish shipyards in Stettin, Gdynia and Gdansk, as the commissars of the European Commission competition policy ordained who could build ships and where. The Gdansk shipyard was of course the most famous, as the birthplace of Solidarity and the rise of a charismatic electrician named Lech Walesa, who took the challenge to General Jaruzelski and the Communist regime, and began a process that would shake the Soviet bloc to its very foundations. Back in the early 1980s, Walesa's work place was known as the 'Lenin Shipyard', and its eponymous main gate, behind which the giant gantries towered, now looked much as it did back then. There were the pictures of Pope John Paul, the Solidarnosc banner and bunches of flowers with flickering candles next to the monument that commemorated the shipyard workers whose earlier revolt in the 1950s had been crushed violently by the Gomulka regime, leaving a number of workers bloody and dead on the cobbles.

Despite my not being able to understand Polish, in my view the mood at the yard was similar to that in the Silesian coalfield, which in turn reminded me of the countless times I have reported from outside or inside doomed British factories and yards. Except here, 'health and safety' wasn't such a big concern and we could get the sort of pictures you simply couldn't get back home. The yard was much slimmed down, and the trickle of workers tried to avoid eye-contact. Back in the North East or South Yorkshire, the appearance of a camera crew outside the gates usually signified that redundancy or closure was around the corner, and it was no different here.

Away from the shipyard was the glorious Hanseatic city of Gdansk, or at least that part of it that had been resurrected from the ruins of the Second World War. (Our hotel was set amongst ruined, flooded basements and teetering bombed-out ruins.) Occupying an office in a wonderful piece of Gothic kitsch was the former shipyard worker who had gone on to become President of a democratic Poland.

'He will pretend not to notice you when you go in,' said Chris. 'He has discovered the Internet in a big way and likes to chat on line'. It was true. Walesa appeared to have two laptops on his desk connected to each other, and he made no attempt to look up as the cameraman set out his lights.

When finally Walesa did grudgingly acknowledge us, he leant across his desk and I shook his hand. After which a somewhat surreal interview took place which sometimes verged on the ludicrous 'The Pope was responsible for 20 per cent of the effort to bring down Communism,' he asserted. 'I, Lech Walesa, was responsible for 80 per cent.' Instead of a vigorous defence of his old shipyard – still one of the biggest employers in Gdansk – Walesa was dismissive of the work force. 'The unions are too militant,' he said. And when it came to the shipyard itself, Walesa was even more dismissive: 'The trouble is that in Poland, the Polish cannot build ships, they have to be assembled from parts that are brought together.' I couldn't help but like Lech Walesa, but the more he tried to sound and look statesmanlike, the more slightly ridiculous he sounded. Clearly he was a national hero for all the right reasons, and obviously he deserved to be treated with an enormous amount of respect.

Walesa was certainly a far more rounded and decent character than the Polish Foreign Minister Radoslaw Sikorski, whom I had interviewed in Warsaw the day before. Off-camera Sikorski's arrogance was something to behold – especially when it came to the Russians, whom he held in some sort of deep contempt. He even managed to refer to the Soviet enclave of Kaliningrad as a 'town full of whores'. I thought: you wouldn't catch old Lech being so gauche. I hope he is continuing to enjoy the view across the old town in Gdansk and improving his grasp of the information superhighway.

Baghdad – and bust

EVEN BEFORE I had met George Galloway, at the back end of the 1990s, I had been warned off him. According to one of my predecessors at *Tribune*, the firebrand MP had once threatened to sue the magazine – which, even if only a threat, was a heinous crime. *Tribune* has never had any money and one successful legal suit could bring the whole edifice down. But oddly enough it was to Galloway that I turned when I received my first libel threat – from the wife of Labour front-bencher, Alistair Darling. I can't remember what we had done, or what we were accused of doing, but Tom Clarke, another Labour MP and long-time friend of *Tribune*, urged me to call Galloway. 'He's bloody good at getting damages himself – and maybe he'll help Trib', volunteered Tom.

George was more than helpful. He immediately put me in touch with the legendary Oscar Beuselinck of Davenport Lyons, who had certainly helped Galloway on a few occasions, but was better known for acting for the late Robert Maxwell. I went to see Oscar, who had an alarming habit of saying 'fuck' in almost every other sentence. It had been suggested that I ask Oscar about his love life as an opening gambit, as this was most likely to elicit the most 'fucks'. Oscar, it transpired had 'fucked' almost everyone. 'I only ever sacked one person, and that was because he was fucking my secretary. Only I was allowed to fuck my secretary!', barked Oscar. It also transpired that Oscar had been an avid reader of *Tribune* during the Second World War 'to annoy the fucking officers'. He had been based in Alexandria at the time of the 'Soldiers Parliament', that had been the brainchild of future Labour MPs Leo Abse and Willie Hamilton. He saw off Mrs Darling, just as he saw off a number of legal threats, and would never take a penny. As did former MP and QC Arthur Davidson, who once told me that he did have one political regret: 'Playing tennis on the day of the General Election.' The day in question in 1983 was also the one on which Arthur lost Accrington by a handful of votes.

I have always been an Arabist, and George Galloway not only touched all of the right political buttons for me, he was and is an orator extraordinaire. In short, as the Parliamentary Labour Party became increasingly filled by on-message robots and assorted drones, Galloway stood out. He was bright and radical; too smart to be taken in by the Blairite nonsense, but not clubbable. He could always be relied upon to give as good as he got – and more, running old enemies such as John Reid in circles. I always admired George for this because he was quite fearless – and in the case of Reid, who was arguably the most intellectually dishonest of all of the Blairites, but who much of the Numpty media used to be in awe of, Galloway could be relied upon to deliver a good old-fashioned Glasgow kiss.

Galloway might have survived in the Labour Party had he been more clubbable and biddable, but that is another story.

In 2002, George told me about a planned trip to Baghdad and a sanctions-busting flight to Basra. It transpired that he was taking a posse of journalists, and from most of the mainstream media.

Would I like to go? Given the now incessant sound of the tom-tom war drums from the Bush administration, this seemed like too good a trip to miss. In fact I ended up travelling to Iraq twice before the American-led attack, on both occasions heading across the desert from Amman in Jordan to the Iraqi border, which was marked by a larger-than-life statue of Saddam Hussein on a horse that was clearly too small, with rocket propelled launchers attached to his side. I often wonder what has become of this extraordinary piece of kitsch. Perhaps it stands next to some large swimming pool at a Texan Ranch. Next to it was a large sign, which stated in Arabic and in halting English the requirement for all visitors to have compulsory HIV tests. Shivers went down my spine the first time I read this stipulation as I surveyed the fly-blown scene, but fortunately no one ever advanced needle in hand.

The western desert gateway to Baghdad was essentially a modern freeway, with picnic spots – concrete umbrellas as it happens – marking the way to the approaches of Baghdad, where desert gives way to palm groves. Once inside the city, it was possible to see the occasional ziggurat and anti-aircraft machine gun emplacements. Apart from a few police checkpoints, Baghdad was remarkably unprepared for what was to come. On the occasions we were stopped, as soon as George emerged in his shades, he was mobbed, and we were soon on our way. All of this made me think that George could just as easily be the Member for Baghdad East. But back then, one of the few ways for Western journalists to get into Iraq was to travel with George Galloway, and most of the British broadcasters and newspapers from the BBC to the *Daily Telegraph* were more than happy to send journalists with him.

The Hotel Al Rasheed was our base, and to get to the foyer, there was no escaping having to tread on a mosaic of George Bush Senior, which is of course the ultimate intended insult for anyone.

On one occasion there was an exhibition of Saddam Hussein oil paintings on easels in the foyer, each one with the then dictator in different garb. He might be playing golf, or he might be wearing a Homburg hat and waving a shotgun. He could be dressed as a jockey or as a musician. Whatever the many identities of the Iraqi strong man, I was intrigued by his serpent eyes. I said to my cameraman, 'Can you get up close, and get those eyes?' He did. Too close in fact: he nudged one with his camera, causing the whole lot to concertina to the ground.

One day that had started uneventfully with us all asking be ferried to various sites identified by the Americans and British as holding weapons of mass destruction (they were, we were usually told, 'mushroom farms' or 'chicken farms'), I was wandering around the hotel when I spotted the then leader of the Austrian Freedom Party, Jorg Haidar. With the cameraman in tow, I asked what he was doing. 'I have come to help the Iraqi children!', he said, before disappearing at breakneck speed with his entourage. In fact he had come to speak at an anti-sanctions conference, which also explained why the Russian nationalist leader Vladimir Zhirinovsky was also there. Beckoning me over, he volunteered to be interviewed and for some reason best known to him, gave me his cigarette lighter in return for a BBC pen.

Back then it was possible for a Westerner to walk out of the hotel gate, hop in a battered taxi and head downtown. Ordinary Iraqis were always up for a conversation, and extremely well briefed as to what was happening in the outside world. The deal appeared to be: keep quiet about politics and the state will, by and large, keep out of your life.

The Baghdad night scene was pretty lively, and in some of the wealthier districts it was easy to imagine that one had been transported to Beirut. The journalist Paul Moorcraft was one of my companions on many of our wanderings around the markets. He was pretty convinced that Saddam did have weapons of mass destruction, and as a veteran reporter of innumerable conflicts was a great raconteur – even if his singing didn't always live up to his boasts. Paul was one of the very few ever to publicly acknowledge that he had been wrong about Saddam's non-existent WDM.

The only people who seemed extremely wary were the Iraqi Christians, who could sometimes be found running shops that sold alcohol. The terrible irony of what was about to befall Iraq was that two avowed Christian leaders, Bush and Blair, effectively signed the death warrant, not only for secular Iraq but for the Assyrian and Chaldean Christian communities – the former the original inhabitants of Mesopotamia who still spoke Aramaic, the language of Christ. Andy Darmoo, an Iraqi Christian whose father had been attached to the RAF at Habanyia in Iraq and whose family had moved to Britain in the 1950s, was on both trips and became a close friend. (Later we set up a campaign called 'Save the Assyrians', with the former Archbishop of Canterbury George Carey as Honorary Chairman.) On one occasion we were both asked over for coffee in the Al Rasheed by an Iraqi in a black leather jacket. He asked me if there was anything I wanted: 'Anything, anything – just ask for it!' Momentarily I thought of replying, 'Well, you know the girl who reads the weather on TV … ', but I thought better of it. All week, some of us had been drooling as statuesque Serbian women dived lazily into the hotel pool – girlfriends, we were told, of one of Saddam's playboy sons.

We flew to Basra in the south in an Iraqi passenger plane, having been warned by George Galloway that this was an infringement of the 'no fly zone' and that we were liable to be buzzed by American planes. Apparently on an earlier occasion, when a US pilot warned the Iraqi pilot of a passenger plane heading south to land or face the consequences, Galloway advanced into the cockpit and informed the American pilot that if the plane were forced down he would have the blood of a British MP and a countless NGO charity workers on his hands. The flight went ahead unimpeded.

There were no nasty surprises for us, except when I looked down at what had once been the great Southern Marshes, immortalised by the travel writer Wilfred Thesiger in *The Marsh Arabs*. For as far as the eye could see, the land had become a slat-encrusted wilderness. A few brackish pools were all that remained of what had once been described as the 'Garden of Eden'. When we arrived in Basra, I asked the thuggish-looking Governor of the province what had happened to the M'dan people, and why the whole area had been drained. 'It has been done in order to build more hospitals and schools,' came the reply. That sounded spookily familiar.

Arguably one of the few positives to have come from the invasion of Iraq has been the flowing again of the waters into the Marshes, and in some areas at least, their swift recovery after British army engineers blew up Saddam's huge dams and dykes. Some of the Marsh Arabs have even resumed their bucolic way of life.

Basra had been a city of canals, but these were largely choked with rubbish. The hospitals however stood testament to the astonishing advances that pre-war Iraq had made in medicine, with some of the best-trained doctors in the world emanating from that country. But this was the time of sanctions. We were told that key cancer drugs were banned or in short supply, that even pencils were subject to a ban because they contained graphite. And then there was the gruesome museum of hideously deformed babies and foetuses, some pictured, others pickled. These deformities had been caused by the Allied forces use of depleted uranium during the first Gulf War, although it was never clear whether Saddam's ruinous war against Iran had been a major contributory factor as well.

The whole sickening scene of a once proud health service on its knees was compounded by a particularly ghastly visit to a cancer-stricken mother and her baby daughter. The poor woman had a growth the size of an apple on her neck, and her pain was compounded by the asinine questioning of one of our number who asked, 'How does it feel to think you will soon never see your daughter again?'

One evening in Baghdad, I saw that George Galloway was holding court with Tariq Aziz, Iraq's veteran Foreign Minister, in the restaurant of the Al Rasheed Hotel. Both were smoking huge cigars, and were surrounded by a throng of Iraqis, some obviously security men. Aziz bore a startling resemblance to the late Peter Sellers, while the sheer length of his time in office was on a par with that of another long-serving foreign minister, the late Andrei Gromyko.

I got wind of the fact that the gathered British press corps was going to be given an audience with Aziz, and that he would answer questions in the Foreign Ministry. So I went to see George, and asked him if he could get me a 'one to one', on the basis that (a) I would write the story up for the *Sunday Mirror* and *Tribune*, and (b) that I could ask him for a message to take back to Tony Blair – which I undertook to do as soon as I got back at the next NEC meeting.

Tribune being what it was, I was the minnow amongst the big boys and girls from the BBC, *Guardian* and *Telegraph*, so it was a particular thrill to get the call that the Foreign Minister wished to see me now, while I was sitting in the coffee bar with the rest of the hacks. The usual Mercedes duly turned up, with its black curtained-off rear seats, and off we sped across the Tigris to an underground car park. Eventually I found myself being ushered into a long room, with two ornate chairs positioned by an Iraqi flag on a stand. Aziz, cigar in hand, got up, shook my hand, and asked me if I really thought that America and Britain intended to go to war. 'I have seen the demonstrations across the world, and Mr Bush and Mr Blair must know that their people do not want this.'

I said that I thought that Bush and Blair were deadly serious, and that they believed his country harboured all manner of weapons of mass destruction. 'Tell your Mr Blair that I have met all of the British Prime Ministers. Tell him I have met Mr Heath, Mrs Thatcher and Mr Major, but I have never met your Mr Blair. Tell him he can send anyone here to look for weapons of mass destruction, and that he can come here. Tell your Mr Blair that we have none of these weapons of mass destruction.'

There was a palpable sense of unreality about the whole conversation. Just as there was throughout the whole of the country. War was literally weeks away, and yet the Iraqi cities were curiously undefended, and Iraqi soldiers would ask politely for cigarettes or give us lifts downtown to the market. And here was Iraq's Foreign Minister seemingly blasé about the prospect of war, unbelieving and naive almost in his belief in the power of democratic mass demonstration – something that was of course unheard of in Ba'athist Iraq.

We stood for a picture – destined for the *Sunday Mirror* – which must still exist somewhere, and then I looked out of the huge office window and suddenly the outrageous vision of American soldiers tramping through the streets of Baghdad came to mind. Pete Norman, then of *Time Magazine* and on our trip, told me years later that Winston Churchill had been the first to try out drones, or unmanned aircraft, in order to bomb rebellious tribesmen. All these years later, and after the end of Empire, the West still seemed to think it could act unilaterally in this, the cradle of civilisation.

The road to war

I DIDN'T BELIEVE Tony Blair's claims about Iraqi weapons of mass destruction from the very outset, and was the first to go public with my very real doubts: on BBC Radio 4 early in 2002, and on the *Jonathan Dimbleby Show* on ITV, where I clashed with former US Secretary of State Lawrence Eagleburger, who became so furious that he started calling me 'Buster!' According to Robin Lustig of Radio 4's *The World Tonight*, this was the first time that anyone had publicly challenged the claim that Iraq had WMD. My gut instinct told me that both Bush and Blair in the aftermath of 9/11 and the invasion of Afghanistan were at the very least exaggerating Saddam Hussein's capacities and were seeking a pretext for regime change. I didn't like the Iraqi regime, but I made it my business to go to Iraq twice before the war began and to the United Nations in New York to gauge opinion and form alliances. As the months went by and the evidence was not forthcoming, and the agenda of the US neo-cons became more stridently clear, I couldn't divorce the political imperative for regime change coming from Washington and London as well as the strong-arming of dissent from the lack of very clear facts.

So I tried to speak with as many people as possible associated with UN attempts to disarm Saddam in the years since his rout from Kuwait, as well as with Middle East experts with long experience of the region. Unconvinced by Tony Blair, I led the opposition to the build-up to war on Labour's official ruling body, the thirty-strong National Executive Committee, which comprises the Prime Minister, leading members of the Cabinet, elected representatives from the Parliamentary and European Parliamentary parties, trade union representatives and half a dozen members from the constituencies. Arriving back from Baghdad shortly before the first bombs began to fall, I said to Tony at the NEC Meeting, 'Tony, you know it is easier to have a cup of tea with Tariq Aziz that it is with you. He totally denies that Iraq has WMD, and wants to invite you or anyone else you choose to go over and see for yourself.'

This was met with stony silence to begin with as Blair grappled with the fact that one of his own Labour NEC members had actually gone to Baghdad and met with Tariq Aziz. He then launched into his now wholly predictable mantra about WMD, before giving me the quizzical eye. Later he bumped into Chris Mullin, former Editor of *Tribune* and later a junior minister. 'Do you know Seddon has just been to Iraq and met with Tariq Aziz? The Iraqis must be desperate!' In his published diaries, Alastair Campbell claims that Blair laughingly told him that I thought Aziz was 'a nice man', but as we now know, neither Tony Blair nor Alastair Campbell make for reliable witnesses.

When later I came back from New York I went on the *Today* programme and said that the view at the United Nations was that military action without a second resolution would be illegal. I also went to see Gordon Brown. Surely Brown would be able to see this? I met him in the Treasury and said to him that any attack on Iraq would probably be illegal, and cost an absolute fortune

(I thought that this argument would appeal to Brown.) He said, 'Well I can't really persuade you over Iraq, Mark.' He then went on to try and persuade me of the benefits of the Private Finance Initiative, as I had been raising objections to the PFI as a member of Labour's Economic Policy Commission, which he chaired. This gave me the impression that Gordon Brown was more concerned about his wretched PFI than the upcoming war in Iraq. In truth, though, I suspected that Brown didn't really support the coming war, but had decided to quietly go along with it.

My own opposition to the Iraq war wasn't based on pacifism. *Tribune* had gone out on a limb to support the intervention to halt the ethnic cleansing of Kosovo, enraging plenty of people on the Left. I even have a letter from Tony thanking me for our support, 'which comes as something of a welcome surprise.' We had also supported former Foreign Secretary Robin Cook's mission to bring an end to the murderous butchery in Sierra Leone. But Iraq was different – not because Saddam Hussein wasn't a ruthless dictator (whom we had once helped to arm) but because Tony Blair was adamant that Saddam Hussein was flouting UN weapons inspectors and had WMD. He was equally adamant, telling us at the end of September 2002 that 'regime change is not United States policy'. But he would not go to the United Nations to ascertain the circumstances in which any invasion of Iraq could be legal.

So years later I sent Sir John Chilcot and his Iraq Inquiry what I believed to be probably the only record in which Tony Blair and various senior government ministers – including John Prescott, Jack Straw, John Reid, Charles Clarke and Geoff Hoon – faced both serious questions and direct opposition to the road to war. We will have to wait another thirty years for the Cabinet papers, and it is doubtful whether a record of meetings from the Parliamentary Labour Party or the European Parliamentary Labour Party was ever properly kept. These minutes, faithfully recorded by the current chair of the Labour Party National Executive Committee, Ann Black, provide a powerful snapshot of Tony Blair and ministers at three key meetings of what is supposed to be the 'sovereign policy making' body of the Labour Party from September 2002 to 25 March 2003, when Britain, along with America, was five days into 'shock and awe'. While the Labour Party maintains a somewhat abridged and pruned version of events, Ann Black's record has never been disputed. On three separate occasions and with the support of three lonely souls – Ann Black, Dennis Skinner and Christine Shawcroft – we attempted to force votes blocking British involvement in the Iraq venture unless it was explicitly backed by the United Nations and in accordance with international law. Defeated twice, and finally blocked by a 'procedural motion' on the third, I walked out of the meeting.

Unlike any of the mandarins, ministers, diplomats and military chiefs, none of us can claim to have seen intelligence reports on supposed Iraqi WMD. In common with those who at PLP and European PLP meetings wanted to support Tony Blair but clamoured for facts to make their case to angry constituents, we did all finally get to read the 'dodgy dossier' that amongst other lurid claims had Saddam's weapons of mass destruction menacing the British sovereign bases of Akrotiri and Episkopi in Cyprus.

Reporting from inside Iraq in 2002, and then on the eve of war in 2003 for the BBC and *Sunday Mirror*, I had told Tariq Aziz that he should be in absolutely no doubt that Britain meant to go to war with Iraq. After days with other journalists being promised visits to sites identified presumably by American and British intelligence as having WMD and being fobbed off with those claims that they were 'mushroom farms' or 'baby milk factories', to me Aziz's protestations had sounded lame. But it was when I subsequently interviewed the former UN Chief Weapons Inspector Scott Ritter, that my own doubts about the veracity of Blair's claims really took root. Ritter, a lifelong US Republican whose reputation was due to be besmirched in the US media by the dredging up of old and unsubstantiated claims of 'improper relations with a minor', effectively silencing him, was clear. Although UNSCOM – the United Nations Special Commission – had been repeatedly frustrated, it had finally done its job. The nuclear programme was eliminated; if chemical weapons still existed there would be proof; Iraq was in compliance with UNSCOM over biological weapons. In any event, chemical and biological weapons have a limited shelf life.

In the weeks running up to the invasion I met with former Czech Foreign Minister – and then President of the UN General Assembly – Jan Kavan in New York. Kavan was in regular contact with his old friend Robin Cook and was clear, as was Cook, that military action without a second UN resolution would be in contravention of international law – a fact finally publicly acknowledged when it was too late by Kofi Annan. That third motion I tabled on 25 March 2003 at Labour's NEC – in front of Tony Blair, John Prescott and Jack Straw – was a joint effort by Kavan and me, with I suspect Robin Cook's knowledge and approval. The second promised UN Security Council resolution had failed, and the NEC motion demanded that 'immediate advice' be sought from both the UN Secretary General and the President of the UN General Assembly 'on what steps need to be taken by HM Government to ensure that Britain is once again in compliance with the United Nations Charter.' Tony Blair, a former lawyer, had argued that 'lawyers opinions tend to reflect their own political perspectives, but the Government's own Attorney General [Lord Goldsmith] has ruled that this war is legal.' He went on to say that 'structural questions about the United Nations and the European Union are secondary to those around future relations with the United

States. Partnership is infinitely preferable to the French desire for a rival pole of power, which could revive the dynamics of the Cold War.' France had led opposition to the second UN Security Council Resolution, and Jack Straw added that 'France simply can't cope with the fact that America is also intellectually and scientifically dominant.'

Tony Blair had desperately wanted that second UN Security Council resolution. Throughout all our meetings it was advanced by him as the reason for not binding his hands too early, as it was with the Cabinet and the Parliamentary Labour Party. On 28 January, after Dennis Skinner had faced Blair and jabbing his finger said, 'This will be the biggest mistake you'll ever make!', and I had argued that the Europeans were demanding more time for Han Blix and his weapons inspectors, Blair said: 'The inspectors can only interview scientists in the presence of "friends" from the Iraqi security service. Backing down over Iraq will make it more difficult to deal with North Korea next.' But he remained optimistic about a second UN resolution, believing that that this would win members over.

Amidst scenes of high tension and low farce back during the September 2002 Labour Party Conference, Blair argued against my first resolution opposing military intervention, except with the backing of the United Nations. According to the minutes, he 'argued passionately for keeping the option of unilateral military action by the United States and Britain, in case other countries blocked the move in the UN Security Council.' I was determined that the Labour Conference would get to vote on the resolution, and if anyone doubted the significance that Blair theatrically saw in this, he said: 'The NEC statement will be studied around the world and Saddam will exploit any signs of division.' An alternative set of words was eventually proposed by the leadership, which stated 'that military action should only be taken in the last resort and within the context of international law and with the authority of the United Nations.' There was a cigarette paper's worth of wriggle-room between resting power with the UN and allowing for more time to get the UN to come around. Even so, Blair's own words on 'unilateral action' should have set alarm bells ringing everywhere. As that debate began with a succession of hand-picked speakers, one of whom accused some of us of being 'appeasers, and guilty of making orphans of the sons and daughters of Cyprus servicemen,' a sweaty Labour Party Chairman Charles Clarke confronted Christine Shawcroft and myself backstage, and asked that we withdraw the motion altogether. We didn't, and lost.

Does all of this matter? The world has moved on; Iraq is no longer ruled by a despot; there are regular elections and a free press. Tony Blair is no longer Prime Minister, and while the promised 'road map' to peace in Israel/Palestine was stillborn, he continues to act as the Quartet's envoy. Minutes of long-forgotten NEC meetings in soulless seaside hotel rooms are probably far from his mind. Yet Tony Blair, the ex-lawyer, rested his arguments on legality, while apparently deliberately forestalling any attempts to get him to seek the advice of those ultimately responsible for upholding the rule of international law, especially once the prospect of a second UN resolution had receded. Sir John Chilcot might have asked a simple question of him: 'Is that because you knew the answer already?' And what of those Cabinet Ministers and opposition leaders who stood by him, some of whom now have reservations about what they did and said at the time; or those, such as Alastair Campbell, who put the 'dodgy dossier' together, or worse still knew what was going on but chose to sit on their hands? Does all the blame for Britain's involvement in Iraq now simply rest on the shoulders of Tony Blair?

Presumably it does all still matter, as otherwise there would not have been an inquiry under the chairmanship of Sir John Chilcot. And it clearly matters for other reasons too: thousands of

Iraqis have died and suffered unimaginable hardships, and while Iraq may now be a more stable place, the bulk of its minorities, including many of the original inhabitants of Mesopotamia, the Assyrian Christians, have fled. Islamist extremism was fuelled by the war and terrorism is more menacing because of it. Britain, sometimes seen as a force for good in the Muslim world, is now regarded in altogether different light.

My offer to go and present evidence to Sir John Chilcot received a polite response, in which it was pointed out that the Inquiry 'thanked me', but had 'an enormous amount of evidence' to sift through, so 'it wouldn't be possible ... at this time,' etc., etc. Same old British establishment, up to the same old tricks. In any event, the Inquiry had been suitably constructed so as to give it no power whatsoever to do anything concrete. Chilcot avoided asking anyone to appear before him who wasn't from within the system – and I include in that the journalist David Aaronovitch, who once promised me on air, on the *Nicky Campbell Show*, that he would eat his hat if WMD weren't found. He still hasn't eaten any hats.

Tony Blair – like George Bush – will of course never be held to account for what is by any reckoning a war crime. But Tony will have to answer to his maker one day, since he strongly believes in one. However blasé our permatanned, multi-millionaire ex-PM can be, I think he has the haunted look about him. What convinces me is that just before the war, Tony asked a friend of mine for some 'heartfelt advice'. The individual was an MP, a former miner, who apart from his Catholicism was about as far removed from Tony's world as it is possible to imagine. The meeting took place immediately before Tony took off for Rome to see the Pope, presumably to seek his blessing for the coming firestorm. So what did Tony want from my old friend? Why, he wanted to hear more about Thomas Aquinas and his theory of the 'Just War'.

'Road map' to nowhere

WITH MONOTONOUS REGULARITY Tony Blair used to hold up the prospect of very real progress in the Middle East as the justification for Labour's – and Britain's – support for his and George Bush's invasion of Iraq. This was the 'Palestinian road map', and much as I wanted to believe Tony, my own experiences in the West Bank and Israel suggested to me that it was pie in the sky. On one occasion I broke the happy consensus at an NEC meeting to say as much, and was rounded on by John Prescott. He was furious that anyone could doubt that since the 'road map' was Western policy, and Tony had committed to it, it would work.

I had seen the reality of daily life for Palestinians on the West Bank, which had been occupied by Israel in 1967 and was supposed to form the bulk of what would one day be an independent Palestine. What I had seen had left a very deep impression, and an abiding suspicion of Western intent towards the Palestinians, allied to the real failure of the Arab World to do very much to help them either. By the turn of the twenty-first century, the West Bank had become a series of unconnected Palestinian 'Bantustans', as more and more illegal encroachments snuffed the life out the possibility of a viable Palestinian state. Meanwhile, Tony Blair was busy making more money, jetting off to AIPAC Conventions in Washington and sounding as convincingly unconvincing as ever.

Back in the spring of 2002 I joined a delegation of MPs and journalists who had been invited by the PLO to take stock of the situation in the Palestinian town of Jenin, shortly after stories had begun to emerge of a 'massacre' carried out by the Israeli Defence Force (IDF). We flew in via Amman in Jordan, with light relief being provided at the Allenby Bridge crossing by Labour MP Bob Wareing. As the rest of us queued up to have everything we stood in or were attempting to carry in examined in minute detail, I noticed that Bob was standing waiting for us on the Israeli side, wheelie bag in one hand, ciggy in the other. 'I just walked straight through!', said the Charlie Drake lookalike.

It wasn't as easy to get to Jenin. For a start the town was blocked off to the outside world, with all roads leading to the town shut down by the IDF. We had to wend our bumpy way through fields to reach the place, and once there, the stench of putrefaction was overwhelming. The town had been the scene of a major firefight between the Israelis and the Palestinians, since the Intifada was still raging. All around there was rubble. Israeli bulldozers had cleared their way into the town, making it easier for armoured vehicles to move. From the vantage point of a heavily vandalised mosque it was possible to see the damage from all directions. While Human Rights Watch later said that Jenin had not been a 'massacre', clearly something seriously bad had happened here, leaving over fifty Palestinians and thirty Israelis dead. The stench was coming from bodies buried in the rubble.

The Mayor of Jenin told us that the Israeli action was very similar to the way in which the South African military used to take control of townships and patrol them. He was also pretty emphatic that we should leave before dusk. That advice was ignored, as our coach spluttered into life and clouds of dust rose in our wake. Before we had made much progress – it was dark by this time – the coach came to an abrupt halt. A couple of teenage soldiers, conscripts as it turned out, were pointing guns and shouting. A military checkpoint was just about visible in the near distance. The standoff lasted a good hour, with the driver finally being frogmarched off and splayed against the wall. Part of me saw it from the Israeli perspective: nervous conscripts suddenly spot a large vehicle making its way through the dusk and dust. Could it be full of gunmen, or carry a suicide bomber? That said, the military checkpoints that ringed many of the main Palestinian cities such as Nablus made it near impossible for everyday Palestinian life to function. We could see people queuing to get in and out of towns, Israeli soldiers making life as difficult as possible. On one occasion our coach excited the interest of a tank, whose turret swung round and faced us. Illegal Israeli settlements popped up all over the place, sometimes simply a cluster of caravans huddled around the Star of David flag.

Years later, the 'road map' in tatters, Tony Blair was appointed Quartet Special Representative to Israel and the Palestinian territories. He did so with at least some opposition from within the British Foreign Office establishment, but George Bush was a more powerful ally. Officially charged with encouraging good governance and inward investment into the Palestinian territories, Blair avoided visiting Gaza until spring 2009. Nor has he managed to use his not inconsiderable influence to force the removal of at least some of the myriad Israeli checkpoints that make life all but impossible for the Palestinians. In the meantime, the Israelis have snaked a wall across the West Bank which ignores internationally agreed boundaries at will.

The accepted wisdom is that it may be too late for a viable Palestinian territory to emerge, but Israel remains a settler state, and one that is finding it more difficult to compromise and seek a lasting settlement, as an older breed of Israeli politicians who have seen active service and who understand the need for peace are replaced by right-wing ideologues. The Israelis could, like the Afrikaners, acknowledge the reality of their position in the Middle East, especially in the wake of the wave of revolutions that have been transforming the region, and reach a settlement. If on the other hand, they allow intransigence the upper hand, at this rate the Israeli state seems unlikely to still be in existence in fifty years time.

Libya: Back to the future

MARCH 2011: PERCHED in the offices of 'Big Think' (I write a regular blog 'As I Please' for the award-winning New York-based website), just up from the Flat Iron building on Broadway in midtown Manhattan, and with Libya exploding all over the headlines, it seems an age since I watched the opening salvos of the Allied operation to retake Kuwait from occupying Iraqis. Then as now, the screens and newspapers were full of pyrotechnics. Then as now, the studios were full of talking heads. The difference in the intervening years is probably the massive expansion of social networking sites and the rise of the Arab media. Yet curiously, as Allied planes struck against Muammar Gaddafi's forces, the TV studios still contained a selection of armchair generals and real generals, all tending to agree amongst themselves. There wasn't an Arab or a representative of the Arab media, such as my old channel Al Jazeera, in sight.

I remember watching the opening Allied missile attacks on Iraqi positions in and around Kuwait in the Foreign Office, having been standing around making small talk at an FCO party. As the attacks opened, the writer Francis Wheen and I were hustled down to the press office to watch the action on the big screen. I remember being largely in favour of the ultimately successful attempts to drive Saddam Hussein out of Kuwait, despite the pathetic cowardice of the ruling family, who had evacuated themselves out of Kuwait City to the fleshpots of Cairo as soon as the Iraqi army arrived. It was only later that we discovered that the Iraqis seem to have been given the impression that the US wouldn't object to their invading.

Now, over a decade on, the curious madness of Colonel Gaddafi had blunted even the most strident anti-war campaigner. And in the opening days of that fightback against Gaddafi's forces, I was back in New York, and getting ready to go over to the United Nations to take the pulse of diplomats and journalists. In the previous week, the UN Security Council had defied all expectations and voted for a 'no fly zone', and giving a much-needed boost to morale at the UN itself – anxious to be seen doing what it could to protect Libyan civilians from attack. As the rain gave way to a soft drizzle, and the tops of buildings disappeared under a blanket of low-lying fog, I speculated on this most unusual of New York days. For a start it was grey and cold, yet barely a day or so before it had been too warm to wear a jacket. But then this time of year, which marks the ending of winter and the beginning of the short North American spring, usually blows hot and cold – rather like Muammar Gaddafi.

Gaddafi had gone from 'most wanted' bogeyman to 'most wanted' friend of the West, and within a shortish time frame. The Gaddafi clan had pitched their Bedouin tent in Hyde Park, London and repeated the exercise in time for the United Nations General Assembly in New York, and the senior son, Saif, had scattered Libyan cheques around like confetti – most notably at the London School of Economics, where the progenitor of the 'Third Way', Anthony Giddens, was based. Hilariously, Giddens had gone to Tripoli and been suckered by the Colonel into believing that the 'Third Way' bore a striking similarity to Gaddafi's own impenetrable 'Green Book' of complete nonsense. I wonder if Giddens, who boasted of his special treatment inside the Colonel's Bedouin tent, had also been subject to Gaddafi's legendary flatulence. The BBC's John Simpson has testified to the Colonel's farting – and I once asked former Foreign Office minister Mike O'Brien if this were all true, during a particularly boring Labour Party meeting in Warwick. He immediately confirmed that it was, having spent an uncomfortable hour in the Colonel's tent, presumably on some mission for Gaddafi's new friend, Tony Blair.

Watching the scurrying shoppers on Fifth Avenue, I recalled some of my reporting and other forays into the mad world of Muammar and his Green Revolution, as the old rascal became a YouTube sensation with one of his deranged speeches set to rap as he ranted and raved under an umbrella.

The call had come from an old trade union friend of mine, Phil Read, who back in the 1980s was one of the mainstays of both Norwich Labour Party and the Trades Council. 'Are you all right, boy?', he asked. 'Do you want to come to Libya with Bernie and a few of us?'

This was in the early 1990s, when Libya was still subject to strict sanctions, and a handful of MPs, including the late Bernie Grant, opposed them. The only way into the country was by road via Tunisia, as a number of Libyan planes had dropped from the skies for lack of spare parts. The purpose of the MPs' 'fact-finding mission' to Libya, was in retrospect, rather dubious – to lobby for the lifting of sanctions – and the visit got off to a poor start, with our progress halted at the Tunisian border for three hours in the broiling sun. It transpired that one of Bernie Grant's assistants, who had departed London in a lightweight suit but who was now sporting spectacular wraparound West African robes, had changed his name to 'Sharka Fela Kuti'. Which was fine, except his passport carried his previous name, and the disparity was causing Libyan officialdom some problems.

Before getting to the Libyan border, half the party was detached, put in the back of a cavalcade of Mercedes with black blindfolds tied tightly. After around twenty minutes spinning around Tunis, the car slowed, and the blindfolds lifted. In front of me was a small suburban house, surrounded by pink bougainvillea and with gun-toting guards on either side of the entrance. Once inside, we were ushered into a reception room with large posters of Swiss skiing chalets and one of the Temple Mount in Jerusalem. At which point Yasser Arafat emerged, pushed a picture of himself into my hands and began speaking for what seemed an age. Animated and by turns passionate and angry, here was a leader as fugitive, constantly on the move and never sleeping in the same place twice. I was to see Arafat a decade on: when working for the BBC, I managed to get an interview with him in the old British fort that had become his prison on the West Bank. The man who had once been so ebullient was now a shrivelled husk, his hands shaking – presumably with Parkinson's Disease – and his manner imploring.

In Tripoli, I was put on immediate standby for an interview with Colonel Gaddafi. 'You must be prepared! This may happen at any time,' my minder told me. 'He may ask you to go to him, or he may come to the hotel.' Having spent a restless day and night waiting for the call to come and the Colonel to arrive, a group of us amused ourselves by pretending to be Libyan security and calling the hotel room of one of the researchers who had come with the British MPs. 'We understand you have been taking many pictures, including of our airfields,' I said in my best fake Arabic accent muffled through a towel. 'It is essential that you will now come to the hotel reception and bring your camera and equipment with you. You must do this now!' This was in the early hours, as we hid in the foyer and watched the poor lad stagger down, looking terrified in his pyjamas laden with camera equipment.

The following day I skipped the trip to the Colonel's bombed-out HQ – the place where family members had allegedly been killed during the Reagan era bombing of Tripoli. Years later, when Gaddafi had finally so infuriated the international community that the UN Security Council instituted a no fly zone across the Colonel's domain, he appeared in the ruins, sitting in what looked like a destroyed car, ranting while holding an umbrella. But then Libya has been a pretty surreal place throughout the Colonel's long rule.

My minder was less inclined to let me give him the slip later: 'You will attend a meeting this afternoon with the man the West wants to take as hostage!' It turned out that he was referring to a Mr Al Megrahi, who had been accused (and would later be convicted) of the Lockerbie bombing. Al Megrahi, from memory, droned on and on. His minders in turn did the same. Phil Read had consumed much of a bottle of Johnnie Walker Red Label, which he had purloined down at the docks the previous evening, and was clearly in a reverie. I guess the meeting with Al Megrahi was the point of us being in Libya, but I don't recall any writing or broadcasting that followed in its wake from me. Both Tam Dalyell, the former Linlithgow MP, and the late Paul Foot were convinced that Al Megrahi was a fall guy. They believed that there was Syrian involvement in the downing of the Pan Am flight over Lockerbie and not Libyan, which made for a change. Since Tam and Paul were invariably right and honest to the core, perhaps it is time to re-evaluate what they said and wrote at the time.

Some years later, I was invited back to Libya at the behest of a friend of mine who was advising the Libyans on restoring links with the West. Bizarrely, it was to speak at a peace conference in the town of Sirte, where the protagonists to the Darfur conflict had been invited by the Colonel to talk peace amongst themselves. I asked my old friend Glyn Ford MEP if he could come, and the pair of us gave peaceful exhortations to a bemused gathering of Sudanese. We bumped into a British diplomat at the back of the hall, who told us that the Colonel's peace conferences were quite regular occurrences; that both sides in the Darfur conflict would show up, stay in the best hotels, rub along fine with each other during the conferences and then go back to killing each other when they got back home.

A few years later and I was back in Libya again, this time writing a travel piece for the *Evening Standard* based on the activities of a small company, Simoon Travel, which was run by my friend Amelia Stewart and was bravely helping to open up some of the marvellous Roman ruins, and much else besides, to tourists. This gave me an opportunity to see parts of Libya that I would never have imagined seeing, including the incredible ruins at Leptus Magna. It was while waiting to be let in to see these – as far as I could see we were the only ones trying to see them – I nearly got myself in trouble with the security men by laughing at one of the typical news reports from the official media. One minute the Colonel was dressed in flamboyant green robes, then yellow, then brown. The news consisted of a whole series of cameo shots of the Colonel shaking the hands of other African potentates in ridiculous uniforms. In fact the Colonel's penchant for bizarre uniforms verges on the camp. This was confirmed when we turned up at a beach one day, to be told that a monstrous building perched near the beach was actually one of the Colonel's getaways. On closer inspection, Amelia and I discovered that the rooms could be rented – that is, aside from one very large locked room

at the top of the building. Eventually we prevailed on an old janitor with jangling keys to show this room to us. Marble floors, gilded mirrors everywhere, including over the bed, confirmed my suspicion that the Colonel liked a bit of 'Bunga Bunga' from time to time.

But was it with women or men?

By 2011, the West's new policy of sucking up to the Colonel had come to a horribly sticky end. Our own 'Dear Leader' Tony Blair had seemingly led the way, although I never bought into the claims that Gaddafi had abandoned his 'weapons of mass destruction' in order to come in from the cold, because, as with Iraq, I didn't believe he really had any. In the early days of the Libyan rising, it was even apparent that the Colonel couldn't crush a motley group of civilians armed with weapons they had pinched from his arms dumps.

As Gaddafi literally rained cluster bombs and missiles on his own people, the only other political leaders to come to his aid were some of the leaders of neighbouring sub-Saharan countries that had been in his pocket for years, as well as that latter-day Napoleon, President Chavez of Venezuela and former Nicaraguan Sandinista leader Daniel Ortega. But what was so disappointing was to watch sections of the American and European Left revert to parochial, reflex form. Never mind that the UN Security Council had sanctioned a 'no fly zone' to protect Libyans in Benghazi and the east from certain slaughter. Never mind that our argument against the Iraq invasion had been precisely because it had gone against international law. Suddenly the UN was barely mentioned, as a lot of people who should have known better washed their hands of the Libyans. Just imagine if some of these individuals had all been around at the time of Guernica and the International Brigades!

The East is Market-Leninist – Zhang Zhijun

SURREAL IS PERHAPS the only way to describe it. There I was sitting in a Yurt in Outer Mongolia, drinking goat's milk with the Yurt's inhabitants and with John Cummings, my old friend who was the Labour MP for Easington. Somewhere along the line we had managed to lose John's assistant, Grahame Morris, who some years later was to succeed him as the local MP. In truth neither John nor I were in a good way – the savage Chinese rice liqueur had left us worse for wear – but if anything Grahame was in a slightly worse condition. Being unable to place one foot in front of another, he had missed out on the 'nature reserve' trip planned by our Chinese hosts, which had been the precursor to the Yurt stopover. As for the nature reserve, I vaguely remembered saying to John through the hideous fog of liquor that I couldn't understand why it deserved such a name: there was nothing to be seen for miles except reeds, and in the dim and distant beyond a huge, idling steam locomotive with two tenders and freight trucks too numerous to count. On saying that, the guide leapt to his feet, clapped his hands and a huge cloud of white egrets took off.

We had been in China for a week or so, part of the 'British Labour Party delegation' that comprised Ronnie Campbell MP, John Cummings MP, Grahame Morris and me. Ronnie famously raised a bottle of 'Newcastle Brown Ale' on the Great Wall of China for the benefit of his local press, while I got myself pictured for *Tribune* next to a quote from Chairman Mao: 'Not a plucky hero until he walks the Great Wall'. Hosted by the Chinese Communist Party's International Committee, as I recall, this smart piece of public relations on behalf of the Politburo had taken us from Beijing to the coal mining districts in the north-west, where Chinese miners had been transfixed by the discovery that both MPs had been miners before they went to Parliament.

Back in Beijing, we were taken as dusk fell in huge shining black and chrome 'Red Flag' sedans to the Great Hall of the People, and ushered into its ghostly, silent halls. We headed south to visit the museums dedicated to the Terracotta warriors and then west to Lhasa and Tibet, accompanied throughout by junior foreign ministry officials Liao Deng and Zhang Zhijun. Liao was a bibliophile who enjoyed his food, so much so that if anyone didn't finish theirs, he would be straight in there. I liked to think that this was all a result of his stint as a Red Guard during the Cultural Revolution. Amazingly, he once told us that he would be sent to pluck weeds from the cobbles of the Forbidden City. 'I used to see him there, in his green house, planting seedlings,' Liao would say of the former Chinese Emperor Puyi – 'The Last Emperor' – then a prisoner in his own palace.

Zhang Zhijun I had met through John Cummings MP in the early 1990s at the Chinese Embassy in London. I was new to the city and keen to be published more regularly in *Tribune*, and possibly even in the *Guardian*. More to the point, I had heard that there was free food to be had on the embassy circuit, as well as the opportunity to rub shoulders with all of the other freeloaders, some who might furnish me with the odd story or two. The Chinese Embassy served the best food by far, and its invitations were well worth the attention of a young ligger-about-town. The tall, elegant Zhang Zhijun was then based at the Embassy, and it had been his suggestion to John that he put together a delegation of Labour people to visit China that had also ended up including me. Zhang must have been a good ten years older than me and he had an utterly disarming way of putting people at ease. What he made of some of the insufferable, pompous Brits he must have had to endure is anyone's guess. Doubtless they would have been horrified to learn that this British-educated Chinese diplomat was not only better informed on British and European politics than most of them, he was apparently destined for much higher things. It is of course the job of diplomats to garner as much information as they can from their host countries, and it is pointless to suggest that one country that does it is any worse than another. I knew that when Zhang would take John, Grahame and me out for lunch, he wouldn't learn much more than he read in any of the newspapers. But I used to think about the investment a country like China had made in inviting 'delegations' over, because I could never imagine the British government reciprocating on anything like the same scale. My travels through China started with John Cummings, Zhang and Liao, and continued over the years as I reported for, amongst others, Al Jazeera, the BBC, *Tribune* and the *Guardian*. When in Beijing, I would always make a point of looking up my old friend Zhang.

One year Glyn Ford and I were asked to go to Beijing to speak to members of the International Committee on the 'Third Way'. There were other European parliamentarians, most of them there,

I thought, for the junketing opportunities. Since I knew that the invitation had come from Zhang and that he knew that I thought the Third Way was a load of Blairite bunkum, I speculated as to whether there was any deeper meaning behind the invitation. After all, I had heard that Peter Mandelson had been over to lecture students about the Third Way, and that the Politburo were quite taken with the whole idea, given that it probably seemed to them to be a Western version of the new Market-Leninist orthodoxy. So if this was a validation exercise, why had Zhang invited Glyn and me? I never did find the answer to that question, nor could I quite come to terms with the fact that sharing our hotel – although not our conferences – were three unsmiling members of the British New Communist Party, a Maoist breakaway from the Communist Party of Great Britain. I sensed that the International Committee's conference on the Third Way, replete a with a large banner, was going to be horribly on-message, so I decided to inject some controversy into my address – knowing that Liao Deng, who had taken a break from a large lunch, was 'reviewing' all speeches before delivery. My forthright declaration that the rights of the Tibetan people should not be trampled underfoot and that China should try and reach some sort of accommodation with Taiwan had clearly caused major consternation. 'This will cause major disruption of the Third Way conference,' Liao informed me firmly but politely: 'Will you please consider the removal of these sections?' Seeing such raw censorship in action reminded me of the infamous 'Speechwriting Unit' at the Labour Party Conference. I buckled over Taiwan, but stuck with the lines about Tibet, to the utter consternation of the Chinese.

But my abiding memory of that rather strange three-day interlude in a Beijing hotel owned by the Communist Party was a rather rushed drinks invitation with Zhang Zhijun. Courteous as ever, Zhang was waiting for us on the top floor of the hotel with an expansive view across the murky city skyline. In shuffled the Euro-politicians, and halfway through the opening pleasantries I detected something new about Zhang. I suppose it could be described as a sense of a man secure in his position, and one whose knowledge of Europe and his own country made him much more confident. And it would be mistaken to conflate this confidence with arrogance: of all the many Chinese characteristics, that is not one of them. I can't remember exactly how he said it, but Zhang pointed to the faltering Western economies and then moved faultlessly to outline the political and ideological vacuum that gripped most of Europe's social democratic parties in the early years of the new century.

His seamless depiction of European decline was juxtaposed with startling clarity as he motioned to the emerging sky line of Beijing, a skyline of cranes, gantries and new skyscrapers. This was all conveyed in a non-hectoring conversational way, which frankly most of the Euro-pols didn't seem to get. As the new century arrived and China continued to grow exponentially, I travelled to the far east of China and to Dalian, then Shenyang and other new manufacturing and software hubs. I knew then that the West was ossified and unprepared for what was to come next. This one-party state may have still officially been in thrall to Mao and Marx, but in reality it had for two decades embraced something altogether new: Market-Leninism. After – and perhaps before – the near collapse of Wall Street and the City of London, the Chinese Politburo sagely acknowledged the deep flaws in the unregulated free market. Instead of allowing a Chinese consumer boom, China bought into America's debt. Today, strangely, it is as if nothing ever happened, and it's back to the freeloading 1990s all over again for the bankers. But the Politburo sits sagely, patiently, awaiting the next Anglo-American meltdown.

Zhang Zhijun is today Executive Vice Foreign Minister and a member of the Communist Party's Central Committee. He is also Secretary of the Ministry of Foreign Affairs. Acutely knowledgeable and versed in the affairs of Europe in particular, he is the living embodiment of what it is to be groomed for leadership from a young age. He has the advantage of experience and wisdom, charm and good humour. If there is to be a benign dictatorship of the Market-Leninists, I for one would be happy if Zhang Zhijun were in charge – unless of course I were to seriously fall out with him over Tibet.

The land of eternal happiness: Inside North Korea

FEW WESTERNERS HAVE ever been to North Korea. Even fewer have travelled widely beyond the showcase capital Pyongyang and penetrated the interior. Hardly any have met with senior members of the regime, both political and military leaders. That I have reported from inside North Korea on several occasions is largely down to former MEP Glyn Ford and to my own polyglot status as journalist and Labour Party NEC member. The North Koreans allowed me unparalleled access, I suspect, because they saw me as part of the 'British Politburo', and in *Tribune* representing the 'official party organ'. If only they knew!

I never attempted to dissuade them from their view, and over time built up sufficient rapport to be allowed to come back after I had left both *Tribune* and Labour's NEC, and on a couple of occasions without Glyn Ford. For his part, Ford had developed a keen interest in East Asian affairs, and for nearly twenty years was engaged in unofficial 'shuttle diplomacy' between the European Union, South Korea, North Korea, Japan and China. For his travails, Ford never received any thanks or recognition – and yet he must have played a not inconsiderable role in helping to damp down a whole series of crises that could so easily have got out of hand.

North Korea remains one of the most isolated countries on the planet. Its home-grown revolution survived the collapse of the Soviet Union despite all of the predictions that it wouldn't. But it has done so at a terrible price. People are shorter, lighter and die a whole lot younger in North Korea than they do in South Korea. Half a century of bristling division has left the North speaking an older, more formal Korean, while Southerners find it increasingly difficult to understand their Northern brothers and sisters.

The North has adopted a system that it describes as 'Juche', or self reliance. The pillars of the only hereditary Communist dictatorship are a curious mix of the old Korean Emperor structures, Confucianism and Marxism Leninism. Against the odds, the North has developed its own nuclear programme and warhead delivery system, and has preserved that programme by periodically playing one power off against another. To me the regime is still the direct result of the trauma of the Korean War, where more bombs were dropped than over Nazi Germany. Much of the North's leadership is of the aging generation that actually remembers that war. I met the President of North Korea, Kim Yong Nam – a tall but slightly stooped octogenarian – on a couple of occasions, and the impression I got was of an unflinching ideologue, albeit a very urbane and educated one. This does not explain how or why South Korea finally emerged from military dictatorships, but sometimes when the trauma has been so great – witness the carpet bombing of Cambodia and the rise of the Khmer Rouge – strange, distorted, deeply regressive forces emerge. This to me is the story of North Korea.

People often ask me what I remember most about my time spent in North Korea. Well, apart from the fact that it really does feel that one has joined another rather surreal dream world, and apart from the shock realisation that on one occasion I found myself actually looking at Kim Jong Il in his platform shoes and trademark dark glasses, there are a couple of experiences that I will never forget.

The first was my arrest within hours of my arrival in the Hermit Kingdom; the second was attending the truly astonishing Ariyang Mass Games. It is one thing to watch tens of thousands of child acrobats and gymnasts perform impeccable homilies to the Great Leader, it is quite another to exit the great stadium, somehow caught up with the serried ranks of the North Korean military in their finest.

There were literally thousands of them leaving the stadium, and my camerawoman and I were amongst them as their medals clinked and their boots struck the pavements. The army officers didn't chatter or slouch, and if ever there was a time to be afraid this surely was it. This being Pyongyang after nightfall, there were no street lamps, just the occasional beam from a passing car lighting up the faces of the army officers, as we walked back towards the city. No one looked at us, and no one said a word. We might as well have been ghosts, surrounded by thousands of automatons.

In his State of the Union address following the attack on the World Trade Center, President Bush had included North Korea as a member of the 'Axis of Evil', so when Glyn Ford asked me if I wanted to go with him to Pyongyang, I jumped at the opportunity. A *Newsnight* commission followed, but this could be a difficult one. I had filmed in pre-war Iraq, but North Korea was the most secretive and paranoid place on the planet. I decided on a mini-DVD cam, and explained to the minders that I was filming the

European Parliament's delegation visit. On the first day, I wandered off towards the railway station, curious as to why a large group of women dressed in kimonos were waving what looked like large red feather-dusters. As I got nearer, I could see that the feather-dusters were actually plastic flowers, and that there was a long red carpet stretching from an ancient olive-green railway carriage to the station entrance. I took out my camera and was immediately arrested by a terrifying female soldier. 'Where is your passport?', she shouted, 'Where is your passport?'

I immediately realised that I could be in serious trouble, as my passport was back at the Hotel Koryo, a futuristic monstrosity of a building that towered over the city. Another female soldier joined her, and they both began yelling at me. People didn't look: despite the fact that foreigners are very rare in North Korea, they didn't dare. As my two guards walked off down the corridor to find a senior officer, suddenly an escape route became momentarily clear, and I legged it back to the hotel. That evening, Glyn and I were informed that we would be 'watching a film', and were taken down to the freezing hotel basement where there was mini-cinema. After having been motioned to sit in two oversized green armchairs and given a blanket each, the credits began to roll. The film was devoted to a visit to a state duck farm by the Dear Leader, during which he would give regular 'on the spot' guidance. It is a huge mistake to make fun of crude propaganda, because the North Korean minders genuinely didn't know any different, and would have taken it as a huge insult, but on reflection the film *Dear Leader's Visit and on-the-Spot Guidance at the State Duck Farm* might have been more watchable after a few spliffs. I must have enjoyed it, because I still have a copy of the film somewhere – with lots of cameo appearances of the Dear Leader at each stage of a duck's denouement. There he is standing talking while officials take notes as the ducks walk around a pond; there he is as the ducks head along a conveyer belt to be stunned; there he is again as they have their feathers plucked – and there he is at the end, still jabbering away with heavenly music playing over, as the dead, plucked ducks, emerge in cardboard boxes.

In North Korea there are no outside broadcasts and no Internet – my mobile phone was taken from me on arrival and returned only when I left – and this largely remains a hermetically sealed country.

On paying homage to the Great Leader, Eternal President, Comrade Kim Il Sung, and other tales

WE WERE TAKEN to visit the eternal President, Kim Il Sung, in his crystal coffin. This is *de rigueur* for all foreign visitors as Kim Il Sung remains the official head of State, despite having now been dead for over two decades. Kimsungam Palace was not only his place of work and residence, but it became his final resting place, with all of the windows covered. Of all the places and the people I have encountered during visits to North Korea, seeing the Great Leader lying in State has to be the weirdest of experiences.

It began as the old Mercedes cars with their curtained-off windows dropped us off at the entrance to the palace. There in serried rows are North Korean men in their dark suits, and separately the women in their kimonos. Every North Korean looks forward to this, their day, visiting the Great Leader. Some will have waited for years. They were all so much shorter than us, and the men sported hairstyles that were common in the 1970s. Silently, they and we stepped forward in single file, to join a travelator, said to be the longest in the world. We all looked stiffly ahead as we passed sentinel women resplendent in deep velvet kimonos each twenty yards, to the drifting strains of music that sounds suspiciously like 'The Carnival is Over'. After what seemed an age, the travelator slowed and then stopped. Now we removed our shoes, donned special socks, and padded across a room to what looked like a glass elevator. In fact it was a wind machine, the purpose of which was to blow away any detritus, hair or dandruff, before we entered what were known as the 'Crying Rooms'. Guarding the way was an almighty white statue of Kim Il Sung, arm outstretched, which we advanced towards in rows of six. At this point, the Koreans bowed low, while Glyn and I nodded so as not to cause offence, but to avoid bowing before the statue. Once past this edifice, we were each handed a small radio device and an earpiece, in order to listen to what is truly the most extraordinary propaganda I have ever heard or am ever likely to hear. The point is that the voice exhorting us to weep at the memory of the 'Great Generalissimo, who obliged the rivers to run and the harvests to be plentiful' and other such doggerel belonged to an extremely well spoken English man, in the clipped tones that would have been more familiar thirty-odd years ago.

Alas, it was worse for the Koreans who have made it this far. Female soldiers were telling Kim Il Sung's life story in the formalised way of public service announcers, while pointing to giant, heroic stone murals of the war against the Japanese and then the Americans. Voices rose and voices fell. There was a sort of enforced passion, but it was enough to have the Korean worshippers in tears, which was of course the whole point.

As we moved off into the cavernous marbled halls, the funereal music got louder. And we realised that we are about to approach the room that held the Great Leader's mortal – or immortal – remains, presided over a by a permanent praetorian guard. I glimpsed what looked like a glass coffin, and as we begin to file past slowly I could see the Great Leader dressed in a dark suit, dark tie and white shirt, lying on his back, the head facing upwards. Visitors to Lenin's cadaver have remarked on the waxy look on display, and Kim Il Sung was no different, although I couldn't help but notice that with his neck reposing on what looked like a small rolled bolster, there was nothing to be seen of the giant goitre which disfigured the back of his neck in later years. Once again, we were expected to bow, but on each of my three visits I have managed to get away with a nod of the head.

The music died away as we moved into an ante-room resplendent with dozens of awards, and pictures of the Great Leader receiving them. The pictures recorded a roll call of the West's bogeymen, although most of them have long since departed: Erich Honnecker, Todor Zhivkov, Leonid Brezhnev – all pictured hugging or kissing the Great Leader. And then there were pictures of him with Gaddafi, Arafat and Castro. As a final flourish, we were each asked to sign a condolence book. What on earth was I supposed to write? What happened if I wrote something offensive – especially as the man hovering behind with the ink blotter would read out what I have written? Alternatively, what if I wrote a whole load of rubbish about how moving the whole experience had been and what a great man the Great Leader was, and the book was one day found in the rubble by the CIA? What then? I went for the anodyne, writing that 'All countries have traditions which are important to preserve.' At least I think that is what I wrote.

To be fair, on occasions we foreigners must appear pretty far out to the North Koreans. On one occasion there were four other foreigners – three men and women – on the flight to Pyongyang from Beijing. Apparently they were all members of the Canadian

Socialist Party. But on closer inspection, I couldn't help but notice that the woman in question had a four o'clock shadow and extremely hairy legs. Once in Pyongyang, it was apparent that the deeply conservative Koreans had noticed this discrepancy as well, but were too embarrassed to say anything.

At the border, we eyeballed the South Koreans and a band of US GIs a stone's throw across the most militarised border in the world. I decided to take a train back to Beijing in order to get a better look at the country. At the station, my minder told me that he would happily face death to defend the Motherland. All North Koreans are brainwashed in that they simply do not know anything different; they are also curiously equal. Heading east to Pukchang County, the formidable Madam Li, county chairwoman, challenged Glyn and me to a drinking competition, and took a shine to the British ambassador. She spotted my musical Chairman Mao lighter and put it in her pocket.

All of this was taking place at a picnic in light rain at a state fish farm, with the inevitable singing competition thrown in. It all began innocently enough – Glyn and I singing the Red Flag, while the North Koreans sang some patriotic songs. In the end we were all too pissed to remember any more songs, until finally Glyn and I were forced into a rendition of 'God Save the Queen'. The North Koreans seemed to like this, as I seem to recall spotting a couple of them trying to sing along.

Up a dirt track – some twenty or so kilometres from Korea's own 'Checkpoint Charlie' where soldiers from North and South eyeball each other and where the demilitarised zone fuses into one – is a hilltop vantage point. Across this eerie no-man's-land, the most dangerous strip of territory in the world, it is possible to pick out the hilltop forts manned by the South Korean army, along with their American allies. On that day, as American B52 bombers headed for Seoul, overflying a 200,000-strong joint military exercise, the silence was being broken on the frontier. As tensions mounted on the Korean peninsula, an agreement that both sides stop the ceaseless broadcast of megaphone propaganda from the hill forts had broken down. Once again, fruitless attempts were being made by both sides to lure one another over, in order to defect.

'We fully expect the North Koreans to launch a test missile shortly,' the EU ambassador to China had said in Beijing. The following day, the North duly obliged by firing off a test rocket. Then, at the weekend, it fired off another – this time a land-to-sea cruise missile.

In what may be the first interview ever given by a senior North Korean military figure, the top soldier in the demilitarised zone Commander General Ri Cham Bok was certain that America was on the verge of launching a pre-emptive strike. 'The US has more than 150,000 soldiers on the borders of Iraq,' he says. 'They have 200,000 on exercise here. It is enough for an attack. There is a way for us to win. But I cannot tell you how we will do so.' At this point he smiled. I say it was an 'interview', but really it was nothing of the sort. We had come to listen to the Commander General in his HQ, and I had put my camera on the table while it was still running. Just to be on the safe side I pointed to it before the Commander General began his monologue, and he didn't seem to have any objection. After about half an hour, the pain in my stomach which had been building into a crescendo took a turn for the worse. I was obliged to go in search of the Commander General's lavatory. When I came to flush it, I pulled on the handle which promptly came off. Horrified at the prospect of leaving behind what I had just deposited in the lavatory, I pulled off the cistern lid, only to find some contraption tied with string. The lavatory was well and

truly broken – and blocked. As we finally prepared to leave half an hour or so later, I couldn't help but notice the progress of an orderly towards the Commander General's lavatory, armed with three brimming buckets of water.

A few days before, at a State Department press briefing in Washington, an official had announced that US Secretary of State Colin Powell would shortly visit South Korea. 'North Korea is certainly going to be a target [sic] – rather a topic,' he announced to nervous press laughter. But war, should it return to the Korean peninsula, would be no joke. The Americans themselves estimate that up to a million people would die within seven days of hostilities breaking out, and many thousands would be US soldiers.

I once flew into Pyongyang on an ageing Russian Tupolev with Glyn Ford and his colleague David Martin, vice-president of the European Parliament. Ford had been engaged, without fanfare, in unofficial shuttle diplomacy for the best part of a decade. His objective, as the war clouds gather, was to get the North Koreans to the bilateral negotiation table, even as the Americans refused to meet them face to face. As noted above, North Korea – or, as it would prefer to be known, the Democratic People's Republic of Korea – had been labelled as part of the 'Axis of Evil' by George Bush. For good measure he also announced that he despised the North Koreans' object of adulation, Kim Jong Il, the Dear Leader and Secretary General of the Korean Workers' Party.

'Upper Volta with nuclear weapons' is how one person has described this last bastion of Stalinism. In a land of stark contradictions, the military can boast advanced hardware, while thousands till the land by hand. Modern but vacant hotels stare out on empty streets. At nightfall, Pyongyang and other cities shiver, while the brightest lights are the headlamps of the occasional passing vehicle. North Korea has the look of the former German

Democratic Republic fifty years ago, and gives the impression that a version of the Chinese Cultural Revolution is still in full swing. This is a country traumatised by Japanese occupation during the Second World War, American bombing and a belief in secular leaders, alive and dead, that verges on the divine.

There is no communication with the outside world for the vast majority – instead a blend of self-reliance theology known as the principle of 'Juche', mixed in with Marxism-Leninism.

On another occasion we were taken off to the mountains fifty-odd miles north of the capital to explore the vast underground 'gift museum', the 'International Friendship Exhibition. But this was after I had finally plucked up the courage to ask a group of four young Poles what they were doing staying in the same hotel: they were in fact the only other guests in the vast echoing halls of the Hotel Koryo. They were each wearing small round Kim Il Sung badges, so I imagined that they might be from one of the scattered 'self-reliance' groups of Kim supporters dotted around the world – mainly in Peru, for some reason. 'Actually we are students,' said the pretty Polish girl. 'We wrote to the North Korean Embassy asking if we can come and have holiday.' Their wish appeared to be the North Koreans' command. Each morning, two black Mercedes would turn up, picnic hampers would be put in the back, and with their minders the Polish students would be off on their state-paid-for holiday.

We set off in our fleet of ageing Mercedes, as the car cassette-player played the surreal Korean revolutionary music and formal singing that we had grown used too.

In all my time in North Korea, we were always assigned two minders, in order that they could also mind each other, and the trip to see the International Friendship Exhibition was to be no exception. Off we went, heading up the empty highway until the land began to be more forested and hilly. Gradually we drove higher, until we came to a stop outside a ski resort hotel, which was unsurprisingly devoid of any guests. But once inside it was time for a banquet, which included 'cooking dog' – although we didn't know it until it was too late – and the most delicious mushrooms and fungi, which we were told had been plucked by the stunning women in pink kimonos who stood around our tables. My mind began to wander. Visions of kimono-clad women fluttering about the mountain pinnacles, picking at fungi, began to assail me. Then suddenly: 'Comrade Seddon! What do you think of Korean goals?' Our host was keen for an answer, so quick as a flash I came back, 'Well there is already electrification.'

'No Comrade Seddon, Korean goals!' This time I burbled on about everyone having mobile phones. Mine host was now getting agitated. 'Goals! Goals!', he said as he gesticulated in the direction of the Korean girls in their pink kimonos ...

The exhibition centre did not disappoint. Set deeply into the mountainside, two massive stone doors gently slid open as we approached. They must have been at least six feet thick, behind which I could dimly see a huge grey and red marble hall. Once inside we swapped our shoes for slip-on socks, and another set of doors opened. Now before us lay a seemingly endless marble corridor, with low lights set to mark the way. 'For God's sake don't laugh,' said Glyn: 'They will get very offended.' To be honest, the whole situation was so other-worldly that it was impossible to have any other emotion than surprise and wonder at what might be around the corner. For the International Friendship Exhibition was in fact a subterranean collection of gifts given to the Great Leader and his son the Dear Leader. Huge rooms branched out from the corridor, which turned into another corridor and then another. I began to get visions of scenes from *Lord of the Rings*.

The 'gifts' ranged from the sublime to the ridiculous. There were the decorated ivory tusks from Comrade Robert Mugabe, and a baseball from former US Secretary of State Madeleine Albright. I asked if there was a room of British gifts to the Great Leader, and was ushered into a small ante-room. There wasn't much to see: a book on the British Parliament, given by a visiting delegation of MPs; a mug commemorating the printers' strike of 1986 from the Communist Party of Great Britain (Marxist-Leninist); and a rather attractive, square porcelain clock from one Arthur Scargill.

In another echoing room, there were brand new Mercedes Benz alongside vintage Mercedes from the 1950s, karaoke machines given by Japanese Juche groups, and bizarrely, whole railway carriages. On the wall there was a map which purported to show where the Great Leader and Dear Leader had travelled by train. Little red lights flashed on and off as if it were possible to chart various heroic journeys to Moscow and Beijing. (The Dear Leader is famously afraid of flying and will only travel abroad by train.) This then was yet another weird necropolis in the world's only hereditary Stalinist state. It was a relief finally to escape back into the light and fresh air, and to take tea sitting in an armchair once favoured by Kim Il Sung as he wrote poetry surveying the beautiful forested mountain scene that was now in front of us.

When the Clinton administration signed the 'Formal Agreement' with the North in 1994, it did so in the belief that the Democratic People's Republic of Korea would go the same way as the GDR. State Department officials even narrowed the year of implosion to 2003. But like the red begonias, Communism North Korean style is of the home-grown variety, and shows some signs of resistance to rot. It is because the Bush administration reneged on every part of the deal signed in order to get the North to shut down its nuclear reactor at Jongbyong that the reactor had been switched back on. Food aid, heavy-oil shipments and the two light-water reactors promised for civil electricity generation had been blocked by the Washington hawks. This may be a development of the official policy of containment – a strategy to enforce such privations that the people revolt. But the shivering cold, often hungry Koreans don't quite see it that way. The vast wall murals that announce 'Death to the US imperialists' have a fresh look about them.

During the 1970s North Korea was the twentieth richest country in the world. Then came the Soviet collapse and a barter trade of an annual $3 billion tailed off to $45 million. Fifty kilometres to the south of Pyongyang, I witnessed the effect of this economic collapse in the dingy wards of Sariwon hospital, a principal hospital serving a region of more than 1.6 million people. In the respiratory clinic was a very sick man with a drip that came from an old green-glass bottle via a plastic tube. Much of the equipment, though spotless, dated back to the 1950s. The hospital manager broke with protocol and argued with the official minder before telling me the extent to which the system was dilapidated. 'Our ambulances are broken,' he said. 'They are working,' said the translator. Two clapped-out Nissan vans that hadn't moved in years stood in a shed. 'Here are our ambulances now,' said the director, pointing to an open-backed army lorry and an old Russian army Jeep. I hadn't been allowed to film, and on that occasion was reporter, producer and cameraman for *Newsnight*. I used the old trick of letting the camera roll as I walked slowly away from the 'ambulances'. In North Korea, 50 per cent of children are malnourished, and in the early part of the decade there had been reports of starvation. Since I had hitched my ride with European Parliamentarians, I was able to follow them to the food distribution centres: holes in the wall handing out rice and corn. This was about fifty kilometres to the south of the capital: of course it hadn't been possible to travel to the mountainous areas of the north-east of the country where widespread hunger existed. We were taken to a local orphanage, only to discover that all of the inmates were twins. Twins are deemed to bring good fortune by the North Korean authorities, a supposition presumably based on the fact that Kim Jong Il was a twin.

Starved of investment, an ancient power station belched steam and smoke from every crevice in Pyongyang. It, in turn, was supplied with coal from such places as the Ryong Dong coal complex, north of the capital. When the electricity failed, the miners couldn't dig the coal, and when there is no coal, there is no power. Six thousand men and women toiled away in the bowels of the earth, in conditions unimaginable in the West. 'We desperately need new wagons to carry the coal,' the mine engineer told me as children scampered through the black mud. There were no visible means of getting the existing battered coal-wagons down the valley other than by hand.

The next time, I had a ticket to Beijing on the overnight train. Glyn had told me that there the train split into three at the border. One part headed for Vladivostok, while another made for Beijing – the third part I would be travelling on, ramshackle Korean coaches. 'Don't worry, the Chinese carriages have an excellent restaurant,' Glyn told me. But he and I weren't to know that the Chinese part of the train was closed off from the rest to stop North Koreans from attempting to stow away. Trying to navigate coaches was like a scene from a Western. At one stage, I was caught teetering between two railway coaches, watching the tracks below, swaying as I tried to hold on. We passed a coal train and I could see a woman and her children, sleeping in a hollow dug into the coal. There was no food for the first twelve hours of the journey, and I doubted that the woman and her child in the coal truck had eaten much more than corn stalks in days, so a sense of realism dawned.

'When we are at war,' said one of my minders, as the train's klaxon sounded at Pyongyang, 'I hope you will come back to our country and see me fight and lay down my life.' With this, he gave the thumbs up, which he then turned into a thumbs down. 'This with my thumb up means you will live! This, with my thumb down, means you will die.'

He cried out, 'Mr Seddon!' I looked at his cadaverous face. And then to his hand. Fortunately for me, it was a thumbs up.

On Keith Vaz and Al Qaeda

PERISH THE THOUGHT that Keith Vaz MP, former Labour Minister and latterly Chairman of the House of Commons Home Affairs Committee, should be mentioned in the same breath as Al Qaeda. But for me the two remain connected, since it was through Keith that I first went to Yemen, and it was through him that I travelled through the town of Al Qaeda on the long treacherous road from Aden to Sana'a – a road that no Westerner would take now. Keith had been born in Aden, and left with his family at the time when the Wilson Labour government acknowledged that the dusty old former coaling station wasn't really worth the life of another squaddie. But I had known Keith and his family from their long involvement in *Tribune* and in Leicester politics. And while Keith would periodically wind up in a spot of bother over something he had said or something that perhaps on reflection he shouldn't really have done, I was, and am, fond of him. He made history as one of four ethnic minority candidates to get elected to Parliament, standing alongside the late Bernie Grant, Diane Abbott and Paul Boateng. Throughout his time in Parliament, Keith has given a huge boost to British Asians and the confidence to many others that they can break through the various glass ceilings that the British tend to pretend don't exist.

During a recent by-election in Leicester I watched Keith in action. Well over a hundred people had turned up to do a mass canvass, and on top of that Britain's first Bangladeshi-born directly elected Mayor, Lutfur Rahman, had arrived with a coachful of supporters from Tower Hamlets – not that the Labour Party nationally deserved his or their support. Keith was in his element shifting people around like great armies on a street map. The Labour Party Regional Organiser stood there, I suspect utterly dumbfounded by the sheer number of people, and probably wishing that there were a hundred more MPs like Keith with so many friends. Ever the consummate politician, he seems to know that a good dollop of charm, patience and good humour can go a long way. Sometimes though I wonder if ge realises just how funny he can be. Laid up in bed in 2010, unable to move following a serious bout of food poisoning, I switched to the Labour Party Conference. Just as I was about to switch over to another channel, I spotted that Keith was in the chair. What followed a was a hilarious romp through what would have been an unutterably boring session, with Keith variously calling delegates to speak in his rather pronounced, theatrical manner. I couldn't stop laughing and later told Keith that I watched him on the loop all over again.

And it was Keith who asked me if I wanted to undertake some reporting from inside Yemen. Given the ongoing upheavals in that country – and the fact that Yemen is unbelievably poor and by most indicators a failing state – you might think that more effort could have been put into alleviating the plight of people in this the poorest Arabic country. Strangely, despite Yemen's long reputation for tribal insurrection and more ominously the fact that Al Qaeda have been active here for some time, the West decided that it was more sensible to get bogged down in an unwinnable war in Afghanistan and an utterly self-serving, illegal one in Iraq.

At the time of writing, the country's strong man President Saleh had been finally prised from his palace by shrapnel wounds to his face. His citizens had been revolting against his thuggish rule for months. But when we went to meet him, he was as you might expect rather haughty and full of himself. Our cavalcade of cars, lights shining and sirens blaring, had shot through the streets of the magical capital of Yemen, Sana'a, and arrived at the presidential palace early. I got the impression that the President was somehow going through the motions as he met us, although he was rather more solicitous towards Keith. He gave each of us a cheap-looking coin in a case, and I asked the President what the coin depicted. 'It is our flag being raised over the British Governor's Palace in Aden,' said Saleh with a deadpan face. So off we headed to chew some more of the mildly narcotic Quat. I do vaguely recall being told by one of the gentler spoken Yemeni ministers that I shouldn't be too offended, but the President didn't like the British much. Nor was I offended, as Britain's doomed efforts to hold on to the Aden colony, including some last minute 'heroics' by 'Mad Mitch' in the district of Crater, were nothing to celebrate. We hadn't exactly covered ourselves in glory in the decades since in the Middle East and the Arab world.

In any event, I have usually managed to hit it off with Arabs, and despite all the warnings about growing hostility to Westerners, the Yemenis were the very model of traditional Arabic courtesy, even though they had alarming looking daggers strapped to their belts. Having said that, the British Embassy had been mortar-bombed and was surrounded by walls of sandbags, and there was some consternation when our cavalcade was hit by a gob of spit on one occasion.

Sky TV and the *Guardian* had commissioned me to report from Yemen, since it was near impossible to get journalists into the country. And that meant that footage of endless meetings and meanderings around the bazaars would not be enough. Fortunately one of the young embassy officials recognised my plight and offered to take me into the mountains to one of the gun markets. Permission had to be gained from a succession of local sheikhs who controlled the road blocks on the way out of Aden, and we climbed into a battered four-by-four ever higher into bandit territory. On one occasion I spotted what I thought was a small valley covered in pink flowers in the middle of the desert, but as we got close I saw that it was a massive swirl of pink plastic bags that had once been home to the national narcotic. 'They're all too stoned and lethargic ever to rise up,' said mine host.

Our driver pulled over and asked if we wanted to wander off into the desert for some target practice with his AK47, but I thought better of it. And so we approached a dusty township, two strips of shacks facing each other in what could have been a set on a Western Movie. Each shack specialised in a different form of weaponry, much of it being smuggled onwards across the Saudi border, for Yemen was and is the centre for the small arms trade in the Arabian Peninsula. This was great camera material, and I managed to persuade the guide and the guy from the embassy to allow me to go into one of the larger shops and downstairs to the basement.

There have been a number of occasions in the field when I have felt my life endangered: in Haiti, for example, surrounded by men who seemingly wanted to cut my throat, and in Pomerania, Poland on the most treacherous road ever. But probably my life was most threatened in this shop. One wrong footfall and I could easily have set something off – not that I was even thinking about the danger of the unexploded mess of decaying munitions. I remember picking up an old Lee Enfield which once may have belonged to a British soldier, and then the shopkeeper assembled a rocket-propelled grenade-launcher, handing it to me and asking, 'How much you pay?'

There was plenty of other excitement as well, not least the delegation's visit to the former Vaz family home and the hospital where Keith had been born. The doctors and nurses huddled round, seemingly awestruck by Keith's depiction of his arrival on this earth: 'I just shot out!', he exclaimed to gasps. Shortly afterwards, at the British ambassador's suggestion we departed Aden on the long, hazardous road trip to Sana'a – in complete disregard of advice from the Foreign Office. And so it was that a motley collection of bedraggled Brits drove through the town of Al Qaeda almost without noticing. In fact I was the only one awake in my car – apart from the driver who pointed out the sign. Sadly there wasn't enough time to stop, and the ramshackle town disappeared behind in a cloud of dust.

When I met Arthur ... and then didn't

'I'M INSTRUCTING YOU in the case, Scargill versus the Pope!' Media lawyer and former legal adviser to the National Union of Mineworkers, Mark Stephens, delights in recalling a recent surprise call from a still impish Arthur Scargill, as His Holiness was being beset with all manner of tribulations concerning his knowledge – or otherwise – of what some members of the priesthood had been getting up to in their spare time. 'Arthur, although many wouldn't credit him for it, has a great sense of humour,' Stevens reminded me at a recent Private Eye lunch in Soho.

Which set me thinking about Arthur all over again. Where is he? What is he up to? And bumping into a Liberal Democrat blogger, of all things, furious at Cleggy's scabrous deal with Cameron and demanding to know why Arthur 'isn't around when we need him?', reminded me of the first time I met this most enigmatic and uncompromising of trade union leaders. When I became editor of *Tribune*, the traditional rite of passage involved two invitations that it was deemed foolish to turn down. The first was tea with Tony Benn – a slightly eccentric meeting of minds in his Notting Hill basement, where I was entreated to listen to a scratchy record of Sir Stafford Cripps delivering a budget speech. The second was tea in Islington with Tony Blair, who seemed to think that the magazine could be recruited to his cause. And I had a third in the shape of a summons to meet Arthur, who then had a flat at the Barbican in the City of London – the 'Heart of the Beast', as he liked to call the place.

Arthur and I met in a coffee shop – he resplendent in Barbour jacket and the sort of blue peaked cap once favoured by East German steel workers, cocked in a rather jaunty fashion. Since this was a few years after the ending of the 1984-5 miners' strike, Arthur was anxious to rebut the Kinnockian version of events which had painted Arthur as very much the villain of the piece. Since I had lots of friends who had been miners, I can't say that I disagreed with him on very much. In fact, having listened to Arthur's forensic arguments, I left convinced that he could also have been a first-class lawyer. Which may partly explain why Arthur still keeps in touch with Mark Stephens and why he isn't averse to taking on the 'capitalist roaders' (as the Chinese Maoists would say) in the courts every now and then, and running them round in circles.

Over the years that followed I bumped into Arthur a number of times and once shared a platform with him on a bandstand in Norwich. He spoke for an hour without notes, made some slightly alarming references to Christ on the cross, and unusually attracted some extra bystanders, including one old bloke pushing his bicycle. Most political speeches tend to have the opposite effect.

So a couple of years ago when I was despatched to South Yorkshire to report on something highly unusual, a coal mine actually being reopened – Hatfield Main near Doncaster, in Ed Miliband's constituency – I thought I would drop by the NUM's rather magnificent Barnsley headquarters, nicknamed 'Camelot', to see if Arthur was in. Now Arthur is 'Life President' of the miners' union, a much depleted band of men, and the echoing halls with their polished wooden floors and silk banners is where he still has his office.

'I saw him earlier,' said the receptionist.

'He has been in, but I don't know where he is now,' said a retired miner who was sorting the post.

But try as I might, I couldn't find Arthur, nor was anyone prepared to show me where his office was. Nick Jones, the illustrious former BBC industrial correspondent, had a similar run of bad luck when he went looking for Arthur a few years back, and others who have tried report the same. His house in Worsborough, it is said, looks a little uncared for – and Arthur is seems now spends more time in France, with his long-time partner Nell Myers, an American socialist who for some years looked after the union's press office. However, the author Cole Morton reports better luck, having gained an audience with Arthur while he was putting together his book *Is God an Englishman?* Cole spent some time wandering with Arthur around the old Yorkshire coal fields, now given over to new hypermarkets, car parks and country parks, where once thousands were employed underground. He found Arthur rather melancholic, still caught up in the times and events that had made Arthur and the miners a real power in the land.

Arthur is of course still leader of the Socialist Labour Party, which he formed when Tony Blair abolished Clause Four of the Labour constitution and set about turning the party into some weird Blairey fan club. And despite a succession of electoral reverses – Arthur has at various times stood in South Wales, Hartlepool and most recently in London during the 2010 European elections – the former miners' leader, now well into his seventies, still won't give up. There are not very many members of Arthur's party, and no one ever bothers to report on their meetings, still less on the party's thus far vain attempts to woo the voters. So I can't help but wonder what would be happening now if Arthur had simply stayed put and not stormed out of Labour? Perhaps with the oncoming monstering of public sector jobs, he might be sought out by a new generation of activists as wise sage? And as the economic firestorm gets ever closer, could Arthur, like Alexander Dubcek emerging from the forests of Bratislava, reappear from 'Camelot' in Barnsley in time for a May Day rally and address thousands of youngsters for an hour, without notes?

Perhaps he will. Because when even columnists such as Simon Jenkins bewail the lack of genuine voices and resistance from the Left, you kind of know that Arthur Scargill still reads liberal columnists and liberal papers like the *Guardian*, only better to know the 'real class enemy' – and to plan his return!

A major miner

A MAJOR MINER. Gone, but not forgotten. Paul Whetton, was a rank-and-file Nottinghamshire NUM strike leader during the great miners' strike of 1984-5, teacher, campaigner and working-class activist. I doubt that he would have made it to the obituary pages of the national press, but then he wouldn't have cared if he had. His death came, ironically, on the anniversary of the day that the strike was called off twenty-one years previously.

I first met Paul as he arrived with a group of fellow miners at Norwich Labour club at the beginning of the strike. Their intention was to close down some of the small East Anglian ports where coal was being imported from Eastern Europe to break the strike. It was ironic then to see him carrying a blue plastic hold-all, with CCCP emblazoned across the side. A broad smile, a moustache, big glasses and a most extraordinarily hairy nose, suggested even before he opened his mouth that he was something of a character. And when he did open his mouth, the voice was as deep as it was friendly. 'Greetings Marra!' was his opening gambit before heading upstairs to plan our trip on an Eastern Counties double-decker bus to the sleepy Essex port of Wivenhoe, where coal was being landed.

Our first outing as flying pickets, in an Eastern Counties double-decker bus, ended comically with us getting lost on the way, finding Wivenhoe but not getting anywhere near the port and spending the rest of the afternoon in the pub. But Paul, and his old comrade Taff King, also from Bevercotes colliery, were deadly serious, and attempts to land coal in the centre of Norwich along the rivers and canals were headed off at the pass. It was Taff who in 2006 told me the sad news about Paul, who had succumbed quickly from lung cancer, but who had at the least the time and sense to record his own message for the hundreds of mourners gathered inside and outside the church in his home village of Tuxford. (When Tuxford had become one of the first parishes to appoint a woman as vicar, Paul's first words were, 'Welcome, comrade!')

'It was typical of Paul that he should insist that his coffin be draped in a red flag,' recalls Taff King, 'that his old Russian hat was placed on top of it, and that he would ask Arthur Scargill to give the oration from the pulpit.'

To be a striking miner in the Nottinghamshire coalfield in 1984-5 was not easy. For a start, the majority of the area union leadership, which had called on its members to continue working, also had control of all but one of the miners' welfare halls in the coalfield. To be a leader of this embattled minority, when all around families were going short of food and clothing, made it even more difficult. Ollerton, which became an early flashpoint in the dispute after striking Yorkshire miner David Jones was crushed to death in an attempt to picket out the local pit, also became the focal point of survival for those Notts miners and their families who heeded the national strike call. For Ollerton Welfare was under the strikers' control, and it was here that Paul and others organised the twinning with Norwich and the vanloads of provisions we took up there each weekend.

After the strike ended, Paul returned to Bevercotes, where he attempted to organise the NUM in the teeth of opposition from both the new breakaway Union of Democratic Mineworkers and colliery managers. He was sacked and fought a long two-year campaign, eventually winning reinstatement – but at Manton colliery in the north of the county, where management figured he would be without a local power base. I remember Paul telling me that he was determined to have every 'last cobble of concessionary coal' that he had been deprived of during his two years without work: 'They offered me the money instead, but I told them I wanted the whole bloody two years' worth.' And so a pyramid of coal outside Paul's house became the talk of Tuxford. He was invalided out of Manton in 1989.

Over his last decade or so Paul helped set up and became a central figure in the Justice for Mineworkers campaign, a constant reminder that many men had lost their jobs and become unemployable for simply being at the wrong place at the wrong time on the picket line. Paul's family must have been proud. Labour MPs, council leaders and former NUM leaders, including Arthur Scargill and Peter Heathfield, were all there for Paul, alongside his old comrade Taff. 'Gone, but never forgotten,' is an easy epitaph to write, but in the case of Paul Whetton it is true. It is also a reminder that real history is often made by ordinary people, who may never be household names, but whose imprint and achievement is far greater than anything from our candy-floss celebrities and our here-today-gone-tomorrow politicians. As I write this, I am looking at a framed picture of Paul, Taff and myself laughing and sharing a beer. Underneath, the inscription reads; 'Thanks for being there 84-85. All the best for the future. Taff and Paul, National Union of Mineworkers.'

Fog on the Tyne

'WHY YOU'VE GONE all up-market!', said Geordie M. as we quaffed pints in the Colliery Inn in Murton, County Durham. Geordie wasn't best known for his diplomacy. I remember watching him once leave the bar five minutes before last orders, and the publican saying, 'Why Geordie, you's leaving early!' To which Geordie had replied, 'Aye, the wife's sick.'

But on this occasion he was referring to the fact that I had 'transferred my loyalties' from miners to shipyard workers and was helping Nick Brown MP with the campaign to save the Swan Hunter shipyard on the Tyne, as opposed to the campaign to keep open Easington and Vane Tempest collieries, which we had just lost: Michael Heseltine had announced his 'hit list' of collieries on 13 October 1992. (At the time I was also helping Clwyd County Council prepare the case for Point of Ayr colliery, so when Heseltine during the course of his speech mentioned 'Point of Ayr – in Scotland', I immediately knew we had some ammunition to throw back at him.)

I had just travelled down from Newcastle with Nick Brown and his researcher, and we had gone to join Easington MP John

Cummings, Grahame Morris and some of the ex-miners down in Murton – or 'mucky Murton', as Cummings fondly described his village. Sitting at John Cummings' knee was Grit, the Jack Russell 'picket pup' whom John had trained to nip the ankles of policemen on the picket lines back in the 1984-5 strike. Grit had gone on to a sort of immorality, after I had composed an obituary to the dog in *Tribune*. In fact I had had to be fairly diplomatic, because Grit had passed away when John Cummings was down in London, and not knowing what else to do, 'Red' Ken who kept John's place spick and span while he was away, put the dead dog in the freezer. I don't think that anyone had remembered to tell John when he returned and went to pull out some sausages from the same freezer …

Easington was 'bandit territory', I had told Nick Brown on the way down, as if he needed me to tell him. They had filmed *Get Carter*, in Seaham, where the beaches used to be black from the dumped coal slurry. John Cummings had been a face worker at the Murton pit, and both he and Geordie M. had featured in some of John Pilger's memorable reports for the *Daily Mirror* at the time of the 1974 miners' strike that toppled the Heath government. I was very fond of John and his agent Grahame Morris. For a number of years, I knew more people in Murton than in my home village in Buckinghamshire, and one of the high points of the year was the annual Durham Miners' Gala, to which, I recently realised, I have been going to since 1983.

As a student I had hitch-hiked up to Easington with a girlfriend to join the picket lines in 1984, and remember a particularly biting January morning before dawn on the approaches to Dawdon Colliery. It had been quite a friendly joust between the miners and the coppers from the Lincolnshire constabulary. But not long afterwards the Met was sent in, and this part of east Durham had become a near war-zone. Out of sight of middle-class England, in Easington Colliery the police went on the rampage, bashing heads in and arresting people willy nilly. It seems ancient history now, but back then a civil war raged across parts of Britain in an intensity and bitterness that the passing decades and grassed-over colliery sites have never really healed.

John had been a reluctant MP, having been leader of the council and a union official, and I don't think that he really ever adapted to being in Parliament. The union had originally wanted him to stand in 1983 in Sedgefield (later Tony Blair's constituency) – and wouldn't history have been rather different had he done so? John had quite a good relationship with Blair, and even showed me a picture of a meeting he, John, had chaired in Newton Aycliffe.

'There's Scargill, in full flow', said John. 'And there's me.'

And who is that bloke grinning ear to ear at the end? I squinted – why, it was Tony Blair! 'Aye', said John, 'that was when he said that Arthur was the greatest living trades' unionist.'

A voyage around
George Orwell's stapler

TRIBUNE WAS VERY much the bit that got away during the New
Labour years, although there were various attempts to hobble it.
The trade unions were warned off from investing in the paper,
and rumours reached me of a meeting in 10 Downing Street in
1997 where plans to try and encourage the unions not to advertise
in the magazine were talked of. *Tribune* has always been run on
a shoestring since birth in 1937 as an internationalist, socialist,
campaigning newspaper, dedicated to the struggle against Franco
and fascism in Spain.

My own time at *Tribune* – 1993 to 2004 – was no different.
Starved of resources, we relied on the good will of supporters and
the trade unions.

Eric Blair – George Orwell – had been a regular contributor to
Tribune between 1943 and 1947, and the idea of regularly selling
off 'George Orwell's stapler' at auction to raise funds was a figment
of my imagination. In fact there were in the office at least half
a dozen staplers of the right vintage that had been acquired by

a former production manager at the paper in the 1970s from a second-hand shop in South London. However, the success of one of these staplers – a journalistic equivalent of the True Cross – at a raffle in Hampstead marking Michael Foot's ninetiethbirthday encouraged me to offload at least one other stapler. Valerie Grove acquired the first, and wrote a furious letter to the *Spectator* when she read that Alastair Campbell was also a recipient of an Orwell stapler. I had quite forgotten that we had sent one to Alastair for a charity football match.

In 1998 Michael Foot was accused by the *Sunday Times* of being an agent of influence for the Soviet Union during his time as editor of *Tribune* during the 1950s, under the alias was 'Agent Boot'. Immediately upon hearing the claim I telephoned the BBC Radio 4 programme *The World at One*, and along with George Robertson, then Shadow Labour Defence Secretary, poured scorn on the whole notion. For good measure I said that *Tribune* had never received any Moscow gold. Michael announced that he was going to sue. He won out-of-court damages and immediately gave £8,000 of these proceeds to *Tribune*; the rest went on a new carpet and kitchen for Jill. Michael's case was directed against Rupert Murdoch, and the courts clearly agreed that as the owner of the *Sunday Times* he could be expected to read what went into his newspaper.

A few weeks later I received a call from Dick Clements, a former *Tribune* editor of twenty-five years' standing. He offered me lunch in Covent Garden, which according to Clements' friends was unheard of. 'Have you checked the small metal trunk in the offices?', he enquired. Dick was extremely nervous that the money paid to *Tribune* for advertisements by Soviet press agencies TASS and NOVOSTI could be used by Murdoch's News Corporation to do *Tribune* down. He needn't have worried – it wouldn't have made any difference, and the trunk had long ago disappeared. To celebrate the victory and *Tribune*'s good fortune, I donned my father's old army Winter Warmer overcoat and put on a Soviet-era Red Army fur hat to meet Michael and others at the Gran Paradiso restaurant in Victoria. Striding through the door, I spotted John Major, having dinner with Richard Ryder MP and some other Tory colleagues I didn't recognise. I went up to him and offered him a copy of *Tribune*, claiming to be 'Agent Boot'. Without so much as a flutter of the eyelid, Major said, 'Thank you very much – I read it every week.'

I first met Michael Foot on the Norfolk leg of the Peoples' March for Jobs in 1983. Although that year's general election was a disaster for Labour, the public meeting and rally for the marchers and Michael in St Andrews Hall was overflowing. But it was at his eightieth birthday party in a music hall in the East End of London that the friendship really began. I had just been appointed editor of *Tribune*, and Michael was incredibly enthusiastic. When I told him that Yasmin and I were about to get married, he gave me the keys to his cottage in Tredegar, opposite the Masonic Hall and a collapsing Miners' Welfare. Michael insisted on phoning at around 8am each morning to find out what we were up to that day. 'Have you been to Bevan's stones?', he would ask.

After finally leaving Parliament in 1987, Michael returned to the *Tribune* office in Gray's Inn Road. His habit of waving his stick around invariably threatened the few operating computer screens, and he insisted on taking the bus home to Hampstead, once being woken up in the early hours of the morning by a cleaner in Stoke Newington bus depot. He took a crashing fall one day outside the office and landed a huge black eye, which he put down to Yugoslav Chetniks.

The big event each year for *Tribune* was the annual rally at the Labour Party Conference – an opportunity for grandstanding,

and an event which New Labour hoped would go away. The rally frequently landed speakers in hot water, notably Tony Banks when he compared the newly elected Tory leader William Hague with a foetus. On another occasion, Banks simply refused to speak. Sandwiched between Gerry Adams and an Ulster Unionist, he thought his court jester act would bomb, and was furious with me for messing up the arrangement (but then I hadn't known that the rest of the *Tribune* staff would demand that we had a Unionist speaker to balance Adams). He was of course right: I had messed up. In the late 1990s the two rivals Gordon Brown and Robin Cook were invited to speak. Brown sent his assistant Ed Miliband along to look up old copies of the magazine, and peppered his speech with quotes from *Tribune* contributors in a meticulously researched speech. Cook, who hadn't prepared anything – and who began scribbling when he arrived – turned to me and said: 'Gordon has come prepared, hasn't he?'

But in 2000 it was Brown's turn to be upstaged. The Chancellor's office called me to try change his speaking time – they were alarmed that Barbara Castle would speak before him, and in time for the Nine O'Clock News on television. Barbara was leading a rearguard yet highly effective campaign to restore her beloved State Earnings Related Pensions Scheme, and was the only senior Labour figure to meet Brown on his own ground as an equal. I had told Barbara about Gordon's cunning plan, but it was only as Brown was in full flow that Barbara's great moment came. Amazed to hear thunderous applause in the middle of his speech, Brown looked up to see Castle slowly proceeding towards the speaker's table. She had splendidly upstaged him.

On another occasion, for some reason Martin Rowson had agreed to emerge at some point in the proceedings, dressed in a white suit and giving one of his excellent impressions of Martin

Bell. The passage of time has rather obscured the whole point of this particular exercise, but I dimly recall some sort of hitch and Martin getting very angry with me. He still does from time to time, but in all honesty I can't remember what the fuss was all about.

I would often drive Barbara home if there had been a function in Parliament as she lived near High Wycombe, not far from where I lived in Aylesbury. If she was in imperious mood, I soon learned how to disarm her, asking 'How's Bertie, then?' Bertie was Barbara's beloved spaniel, and mention of his name would immediately change her mood. Barbara told me she preferred me driving her to her near neighbour Baroness Ann Mallalieu – daughter of the veteran Tribunite JP Mallalieu: 'She's obsessed with fox hunting, dear. I simply cannot stand the continued arguing over it.' Barbara's ninetieth birthday party was held at the home she once shared with husband Ted – Hell Corner Farm in Ibstone, Buckinghamshire – and had all of Labour's chieftains present, except for Tony Blair, whom she had decided was an inappropriate leader of the Labour Party.

Neil Kinnock gave a typically warm speech, and then it was Barbara's turn. Once again she castigated Gordon Brown for his pensions policy, leaving the Shadow Chancellor squirming with embarrassment, and reminded the 100 or so guests, including another neighbour John Mortimer, that she had employed Jack Straw all those years ago as a researcher on account of his 'low cunning'. Jack Straw was there too, but when I looked to see what his reaction was, I couldn't spot him.

Barbara would often remonstrate with me over *Tribune* for not being tough enough on the government, summoning me once to the upstairs 'Tom Driberg Memorial Suite' in the Gay Hussar, along with Ian Aitken, Terence Lancaster, Julia Langdon and others. She instructed me to redesign the magazine and told Ian

Aitken that he had to start writing for it again – which he did, and still does to this day. Only the *Guardian* could fail to recognise the wisdom and wit of some of its veteran contributors. The *Telegraph* would venerate them.

The Gay Hussar restaurant in Greek Street had been the traditional haunt of the Tribunite left since the 1950s – according to Leo Abse, it was cheaper than the White Tower restaurant off Park Lane, and in any event, Michael Foot and others didn't really have very good table manners. I had been taken there by Ian Aitken immediately prior to joining *Tribune*, thus fulfilling a long held ambition, since *Private Eye* was full of anecdotes about Roy Hattersley and the Gay Hussar.

I immediately fell in love with the place, and decided that it would be the venue for our regular *Tribune* dinners and sundry plotting meetings. Amongst our guests was Mo Mowlam, then Northern Ireland Secretary, who put her napkin on her head when *Tribune* columnist Hugh MacPherson began castigating her over Blair and New Labour and refused to remove it. Despite warnings from the manager about the chillies being on the table for decoration and no other purpose, Mo made a bracelet out of some of them and then touched her eye. She then spent the rest of the evening in the Ladies, dabbing her eyes and fending off interested American tourists.

The late Lord Rothermere, fabled newspaper proprietor, came to dinner in 1997. I had invited him after a lengthy correspondence resulting from Cassandra's attack on him in *Tribune*. Rothermere upbraided me for suggesting English translations for various Hungarian dishes, telling us all in a loud voice that his family had ruled the country for many generations. When asked by Martin Rowson if he had ever fired any of his editors, Rothermere explained that he was powerful enough to do so only 'Up to a point Lord Copper' – to which an exasperated Rowson countered, 'But

you are Lord Copper!' As if by magic, a slightly tired and emotional *Observer* columnist Nick Cohen staggered up to Rothermere and planted a kiss on his cheek.

Rothermere insisted on driving Michael Foot back to the Ritz for a nightcap in his Bentley – but didn't extend the invitation to Ken Livingstone.

My friendship with Rothermere blossomed. He would invite me to lunch in his his top-floor suite in the Ritz, where I challenged him to allow the unions back in to the *Daily Mail*. We discovered a shared interest in Tibet: I had been there, and Rothermere pronounced himself a Buddhist. Having finally concluded that Rothermere was another Beaverbrook – i.e., generous to a fault to left-wing journals fallen on hard times – I decided to ask him for some money for *Tribune*. Sadly, on the day I prepared to book our next lunch it was announced that he had died.

John Platts-Mills QC was another wealthy individual whom Hugh Macpherson and I enticed to lunch. He left us to pay the bill, murmuring something about having 'lots of grandchildren'.

Ken Clarke came to dinner and pronounced that he was amazed that Gordon Brown was keeping to Tory spending plans for the first two years of the Labour government. 'We all thought he was doing it just to get though the election,' he said. 'In any event, I wouldn't have stuck to them myself.' Clarke appeared defensive to begin with and remarked that he couldn't believe how disputatious we all were – in other words, why we wouldn't hang on his every word in a respectful silence. 'Do you people spend all of your time arguing with each other?', I remember him saying.

Such was the legendary hospitality of the restaurant that on one occasion the manager Jon Wrobel laid out two beds under a table for me and Labour MP Tom Watson after an extremely tired and emotional lunch which had left us both essentially incapacitated. I

had another function that same evening and vaguely recall Wrobel appearing with a glass of champagne and some fresh garden mint, with the instruction, 'Chew this and drink at the same time.' John, who is from Wroclaw in Poland, must have remembered this magic cure from back home. And it worked. So much so that I was able to stand up, walk straight down the stairs and greet *Tribune*'s UN correspondent Ian Williams who had just flown in from New York. Then we started all over again. I suspect I must have mentioned this tale to rather too many people, as it emerged in one of the newspapers. Vengeance was as understandable as it was swift, and if must have come from Tom. Apparently at one stage in the lunchtime proceedings I had attempted to leave the upstairs room and emitted a mighty multi-coloured yawn down the stairwell. Still, I comforted myself, this wasn't as bad as the senior TV executive who once left one of our lunches at the Gay Hussar and honked up all over his trousers in the taxi on his way back to work.

Talking of trousers, Wrobel tells a wonderful story involving the trousers of the late Lord Longford. As the years advanced, Frank, as he was known to us all, stopped using his knife and fork and started using his hands. On one occasion, Wrobel became rather concerned since Frank had managed to drop his potatoes back into his gravy so many times that he had splattered his trousers. Seizing his opportunity as Longford staggered to the exit, the manager of the Gay Hussar bent down and began to brush his trousers – at which point they gave way and fell to the ground. A passing cabbie added to chaos of the situation shouting at Wrobel and Longford, 'You dirty bastard!'

On the day I read that Longford finally passed away, I went to the Gay Hussar and said to Wrobel: 'Trousers at half mast. Sad news. Lord Longford is no longer with us!' At which point an elderly man in the corner of the restaurant emitted an involuntary sob. 'Sssshhhh', said Jon. 'He was Frank's Private Secretary, and they were supposed to have had lunch today.'

The restaurant is deservedly known as the Left's cafeteria, and for some years it was my second home – especially as I had an expense account courtesy of the *Evening Standard*'s Londoners' Diary. It is living testament to a truth not well known that there was, and still is – just – a British Left that is as Rabelaisian as it is rebellious. The hand-drawn portraits of many of the good and the bad of British left-wing politics and journalism grace the Gay Hussar's walls, courtesy of Martin Rowson. I suspect that he may have done himself some liver damage over the years in drawing this remarkable collection, but I bet it has been worth it.

Astonishingly, the Gay Hussar faced closure in 1999, so an emergency committee was convened comprising Michael Foot, the veteran journalist Geoffrey Goodman and myself, and we met with the restaurant's owner Roy Ackerman to persuade him to lift the axe. The campaign contributed to saving the Gay Hussar and solicited an interesting anecdote from Ackerman. We were talking about the late Lord Rothermere when Roy volunteered that he had met his Lordship at a party once. A few days later he was somewhat surprised to receive an invitation to lunch. 'Vere Rothermere wanted to talk about sailing in the Bay of Biscay, and there was nothing I could do to get him to change the subject. For some reason he thought that I knew all there was about sailing, which is very odd as I have never been sailing.'

Ackerman's usual attire was a double-breasted blazer with brass buttons, which he had been wearing when he first met Lord Rothermere. The explanation made sense. Rothermere had taken one look at Ackerman's nautical blazer and reached the mistaken conclusion that he was a sailor.

On falling foul of Sir Jams

EVERY EDITOR WHO has ever heard the words 'Carter' and 'Ruck' mentioned in connection with a waiting telephone call will know the feeling. I received a number of legal threats during my years at the helm at *Tribune*, but none made my stomach churn quite as much as the one that came on behalf of the late Sir James Goldsmith.

The Labour MEP Glyn Ford had written a fairly excoriating piece about Sir James, and production manager George Osgerby had with customary flair given it the title, 'Today Europe, Tomorrow the World!' Libel lawyer Peter Carter-Ruck stated in his letter to me that Goldsmith was furious because this made him out to be a Blackshirt, and as such wanted an apology and compensation.

I explained that we had no money at all, and then sat back wondering what I would do if he came after my house? The message must have been communicated back, because the following instruction was issued: 'You will apologise to Sir James. You will read and review his book *The Trap* and you will carry an interview with Sir James in *Tribune*.' A courier duly arrived at Gray's Inn Road with a copy of *The Trap*, and I prepared to go and meet Sir Jams in Knightsbridge. I arrived at his rather sumptuous town house to be greeted with a frock-coated butler, and was ushered upstairs, where Sir Jams, like Blofeld, was ensconced on a long sofa. He was accompanied by a couple of young men in pin-striped suits who made it clear by their disdainful looks that I might just as well be something that one occasionally finds on one's shoe, and which is really rather unpleasant on a warm day.

That said, the interview seemed to progress quite well, and having read *The Trap*, I realised that Sir Jams and I did agree about one thing – namely the hugely destructive powers of monopoly capitalism.

Everyone seemed to be quite surprised to hear that Sir Jams had been interviewed in *Tribune* of all places, but even better *The Times* asked to run a part of it, writing out a cheque to *Tribune* in the process.

When I recently told this tale to Goldsmith's son Zac, now an MP, the affable chap seemed almost apologetic. 'Don't worry,' I said, 'it all turned out fine – in fact *Tribune* seemed to do quite well out of the whole affair.' I then watched Zac as he gave a speech in favour of a referendum on membership of the European Union. Astonishingly, he had a hole in his jacket sleeve and his shoes had seen better days. But then Zac is an altogether unassuming but charming man. He is a good communicator too, and with a bit more confidence could probably achieve far more in politics than his rumbustious father managed.

Inside the machine –
The Central Committee

ABOUT THE ONLY memorable thing that Piers Morgan has ever said is that 'Politics is like show business for ugly people' – although he pinched that from Texas lobbyist Bill Miller. When I was growing up, and managed to get to my first Labour Conference in 1978, the annual contest for what was termed Labour's ruling National Executive Committee was a hard-fought affair. The NEC – or 'Executive', as John Prescott would describe it – contained the party leader, who each month would be obliged to give his report, whether in or out of government, and face questions afterwards. Other members included the deputy leader and elected representatives from the Parliamentary party – and later the European party. It also contained a powerful trade union section, one of whose members would inevitably be elected NEC chair each autumn. And then there were the constituency representatives – traditionally MPs, whose election each September conference would give an indication of how far to the left or right the party was heading. Back in the late 1970s, the Left dominated the NEC. I grew up with names such as

Tony Benn, Joan Maynard (nicknamed 'Stalin's Granny' by sections of the media), Frank Allaun, Eric Heffer and Ian Mikardo. All of these MPs were grounded in 'The Movement' and could be relied upon to give a good account of themselves in Parliament and out. They tended to be powerful public speakers, and would clock up hundreds of miles each year speaking in drafty Labour and union halls to members of what was still quite a large living entity of a party.

NEC meetings could become passionate and heated. Neil Kinnock once told me the story of how during one meeting, an argument between right-winger John Golding and left-winger Eric Heffer got out of hand. 'They started to push each other about, grabbing at each other's lapels, so I was forced to intercede,' Neil recalled. 'They both were trading insults and challenging each other – until Eric said "That's it! I'm leaving." He stormed off – and straight into a broom cupboard, only to emerge looking sheepish. He then resumed his seat.'

During Neil Kinnock's tenure as Labour leader, the Left was in retreat. Increasingly the unions elected people to the NEC who could usually be counted on to support the leader. By the time Tony Blair was elected leader, what had become known as the 'Hard Left' was still retreating. The first major upset though occurred in Blair's first year as leader, when Ken Livingstone beat Peter Mandelson for a place in the constituency section. This is probably what settled the fate of the NEC. As part and parcel of the euphemistically described 'Partnership in Power', MPs were banned from standing for election. The annual beauty contest for ugly people was to be no more. Instead, the plan was to allow ordinary party members to stand – the idea being that they weren't so prominent and that there would be less media interest in NEC elections, and less of a chance for 'Mr Tony' to be embarrassed.

Which of course presented an opportunity for people like me, and for the recently disbarred candidate from Leeds North West, the lawyer Liz Davies. I knew Liz vaguely, through her partner, the author, writer and American socialist Mike Marqusee. Liz was, I suppose a typical North London Labour left-winger – very capable and principled, but who had somehow become the litmus test for Tony Blair and his perceived control over the Labour Party. Liz had been drummed out of the Leeds constituency for which she had been selected fair and square, and then was denounced at a Labour Conference by, of all people, Clare Short. I still remember Liz leaving the hall, as the full impact of that speech hit her, and seeing her being pursued by the media. I could understand why Clare and others would feel the need to take against the Militant Tendency and its supporters, but by this stage the 'Milis' had long since disappeared. In any event, the idea that Liz Davies was some sort of mad Trotskyite was well off the mark. I decided to run for a place on the NEC with her, and with other left-wingers Pete Willsman, Christine Shawcroft and Cathy Jamieson (now an MP) from Scotland as part of the 'Grassroots Alliance'. The great guru and organiser of this seemingly madcap charge against the guns was Tim Pendry, a relative of the former Labour MP Tom Pendry, who had been a luminary in Labour Solidarity and the Labour Finance and Industry Group, two organisations traditionally associated with the Labour Right. Tim had rapidly become disillusioned by what he saw as the new Blairite wing of the party's contempt for the party and its democratic structures.

I told *Newsnight* political editor Michael Crick at a *Private Eye* lunch in the Coach and Horses in Soho that this was what I was planning to do. He cautioned against it, saying that he had heard that the Blairite forces, under the command of the doughty party General Secretary Margaret McDonagh, would probably succeed in stopping us.

Crick was partly right. The party machine mobilised to stop us, particularly mindful of how the media would play the election of Liz Davies, given her defenestration on the orders of Tony Blair. They threw plenty of resources at us, using front organisations like the New Labour group Progress, funded by Lord Sainsbury, to produce voluminous amounts of publicity for our opponents. A phone-bank was set up and apparently masterminded by Lord Bassam, who as a plain 'Steve' had once been a militant squatters' leader in Brighton.

That all five of us won – and that I gained the most votes of any candidate – is testament both to the hard work of Tim Pendry and the truculence of a Labour Party which had decided that it wanted to hold Tony Blair to some form of account. The BBC sent a recording truck to our home near Buckingham, and I recall giving an interview in an old Arran sweater, and saying boldly, 'Tony, this is what is called democracy!'

NEC meetings could be interminably boring and long; they could also be hugely entertaining and very revealing. John Prescott, for instance, who was often grumpy and sparring for a scrap, would come into his own when 'the Leader' was away, and he had to deliver the 'Leader's report'. Prescott's reports were invariably streams of consciousness, punctuated with, 'But as you know, JP really thinks that …', in order to put some distance between him and some calumny from the Blairistas – whom the union members by and large didn't much like but went along with. On one occasion I watched as one of the party staffers simply gave up trying to keep up with JP, and quietly put away her pen. I imagine that reports of JP's ramblings must have drifted back to Number 10, because at one NEC meeting he turned up somewhat chastened and read a clipped, colourless report from a piece of paper without any of the old JP chutzpah and bravura.

I sat next to Dennis Skinner, who was regularly elected by the Parliamentary Labour Party. The great thing about Dennis was that he was completely unafraid, and when he spoke, every NEC member, however on-message, would listen to him, nod in agreement, and then vote against him. Dennis usually spoke extraordinary common sense, and actually had a good relationship with Tony Blair, who would have him round to Downing Street on a regular basis. I think that this was partly because Dennis could speak truth to power, but also because Blair was terrified that Dennis would one day blow up. Dennis also liked to be loved, and I was somewhat surprised to learn years later that he regularly reported back from the NEC to Alastair Campbell. But Dennis would go in to Downing Street via the tradesman's entrance and then regale me with what he had said to Tony. It might be: 'I told him that the pensioners deserved more,' or it could be, 'I told him to stand up and be counted over Post Office privatisation.'

I suspect that Blair would probably agree with Dennis in the same way that the NEC always agreed with Dennis. During one particularly dull NEC meeting, I nudged Dennis and dared him to ask Tony a question in 'New Labour-speak'. He looked at me askance, to the extent that I thought I had probably pushed it too far. He then cleared his throat, looked at Blair and said: 'When are we going to apply blue sky thinking to the Third Way approach to beacons of excellence at a local municipal level?' The ensuing silence was broken only by the sound of a shocked looking Blair scribbling ferociously, presumably thinking, 'What's come over Dennis?'

When recently I saw Dennis at Prime Minister's Question showing the rest of the PLP how to behave like an opposition, and David Cameron's rejoinder that he 'should go back to dinosaur land,' I was furious. Cameron is fairly typical of his class and background:

arrogant and largely devoid of any defining personality. His type used to be described as 'chinless wonders'. Up until this point, I had tended to avoid having any serious opinions about him at all. But the attempted put-down of Dennis Skinner not only showed a total lack of respect – Dennis wanted to know how Cameron could defend the exponential growth in the number of super-rich, while the disabled were protesting their benefits being cut – but it also showed callowness. Dennis Skinner, veteran Parliamentarian, a former pit man experienced in real life, versus David Cameron, an old Etonian, who apart from a stint as a Director of Communications at Carlton has arguably never had a real job in his life.

One NEC meeting I do recall quite vividly, because for some remarkable reason Margaret McDonagh (or the 'Ice Queen' as Peter Willsman and I described her) simply lost control of the agenda. This was the woman I recall who had once told fellow NEC member Liz Davies when challenged without a blink of her eye, 'It is a rule, but it isn't written down. The reason that the agenda became unstuck had something to do with Rodney Bickerstaffe and his Unison union delegation. The mists of time have drifted over the exact dispute: it could have been that the party simply could not get Rodney to agree to some policy over pensions or the PFI. Rodney, who had risen up through the ranks of the old NUPE (National Union of Public Employees) was a veteran of public-sector wage freezes, and once told me outside the Brighton Conference Centre that he thought history might repeat itself and once again the government would target the low paid, and he would find himself in conflict with it.

Either way, it became apparent that not only was the NEC meeting going to go straight through lunch, we mightn't be ready to troop back onto the conference platform at the start of business in the afternoon.

As the meeting dragged on, Dennis Skinner became restless. 'What's the matter Dennis?', boomed Mo Mowlam from across the table: 'Need a wazz?' Skinner ignored her. Then the Chair, a marvellous trade union official and Brent Council dinner lady Mary Turner, leant forward. 'Conference is about to start. We can't stay here any longer! The press are now outside the door, demanding to know what the hell is going off!' And then someone suggested that the whole NEC exit through a side door to avoid the press and make a run for it. And so we did, all thirty or so of us including Cabinet members, scampering through the kitchens of the Metropole Hotel and out round the back, past the bins and then into a back door of the conference centre.

Later that afternoon I was minding my own business in the section of the hall reserved for the NEC, when Margaret McDonagh came by. 'At least you look presentable', she said. 'Can you go and join the conference platform?' I noticed that one or two gaps had appeared in the line-up, and obviously this didn't look too good on the television. There was a debate on the Post Office, and when the then leader of the Communications Workers' Union Derek Hodgson got up to savage plans to part-privatise the Post Office, I stood up alongside many of the delegates to give him what I thought was a well deserved standing ovation. But as I stood up, I noted to my alarm that I was the only one on the platform doing so. This prompted the immediate re-appearance of Margaret McDonagh: 'You need to remember to sit when we sit, and stand when we stand. Now go back to where you came from!' A better example of New Labour control-freakery it is difficult to imagine.

But then my conference pass did allow me to wander around backstage. Earlier in the week, we had all been sitting there when it was announced that there would be a debate on the NEC recommendations contained in 'Partnership in Power'. This was odd, because I didn't recall us ever seeing the report in question, which was verified by Ian McCartney (then an ordinary member of the NEC from the PLP section) when I asked him. There then followed a succession of oddly on-message speakers, invariably well dressed young women. Only one speaker – called Frank – was summoned by the Chair to speak against, but it soon became obvious why. He was dressed in grubby shorts and a tee-shirt, and even though poor old Frank didn't realise it, he had been selected to remind the media why Labour had had to reinvent itself.

The 'debate' over, I wandered around the back of the conference centre, where I came across a group of young party workers busying themselves over their screens. 'What are you doing?', I asked one young enough and new enough not to know me. 'Oh, we're the Speechwriting Unit,' she replied. This then is what had happened to the annual parliament of the Labour Party. Speakers were selected, groomed, delivered a speech and then chosen to deliver it by an on-message Conference Chair. And all because back in the old days the delegates would sometimes vote against the leadership for nuclear disarmament, or whatever. This discovery I found the most depressing of all. If professional politicians could manipulate at this level, what were they capable of doing elsewhere?

'Partnership in Power' was a classic exercise in managerial centralism. Labour's federal democracy was turned on its head, and power was transferred up the line to something called the 'Joint Policy Commission', which was supposedly fed into by something called the 'National Policy Forum'. Most of the hacks were too lazy to enquire just what all of this meant – untrammelled power for Tony Blair and his supporters – but it was a system of centralised control more befitting an old-style Stalinist Communist Party. Its real intention was to marginalise and drive out dissent. In the future, policy would be made by two people – TB and GB. And then I was leaked a copy of the report that had been drawn up as a 'command-and-control' mechanism for the Labour Party to adopt, apparently by none other than John Birt, friend of Peter Mandelson and then Director General of the BBC. The Londoners' Diary in the *Evening Standard* published my story, but no one else was particularly interested. I'm still amazed that a sitting Director General of the BBC could have been that close and involved in the internal affairs of a political party. But the problem always was – and is – that much of the media cannot see beyond the Westminster beltway. It is so caught up with the goings-on at the top that it has quite missed out on the fact that today Britain has the smallest number of people anywhere in Europe who are actually members of a political party. In fact the media largely goes along with the fiction that we have political parties, when in truth for the most part they all but ceased to be living organisms, active in their communities and actually helping to make policy, many years ago.

Still, Tony Blair and his pals wouldn't always have it their way, even if they had more less neutered the conference. One year we had an NEC awayday at a TUC centre in North London. This was in the middle of a dispute with the fire-fighters, and of course Tony Blair and New Labour were busy showing just how tough they could be with a bunch of workers who risk their lives each time they are called out, and who helped fund the Labour Party through their subscriptions. In taking to Fire Brigades Union President Mick Shaw over a resolution a bunch of us were going to put down in support, I mentioned our awayday, and suggested that some his members might like to come over and serenade Tony Blair and his entourage as they arrived for the meeting.

I knew when Tony had arrived because a barrage of klaxon horns went off. His desperate attempts to find other entrances to the conference centre all failed miserably, as there were firefighters marking each one. When he finally got into the meeting, he appeared flustered and looked at me with a strange glint in his eye. Apparently when the meeting came to an end, Blair and his entourage headed back to London but got caught up in traffic, coming to an alarming halt outside a fire station. 'One of them stuck a finger up at my members!', Mick Shaw later told me.

Another year during the Labour Party Conference, after a fairly raucous evening in the conference hotel during which the cartoonist Martin Rowson had asked *Sun* editor David Yelland if he could draw Manhattan's Twin Towers on his head, I decided to treat Martin and journalist Nyta Mann to a tour around the back rooms of the conference centre. During the course of this drunken stagger, we came across the Leader's dressing room, which for some reason particularly excited Martin – as he has related in the Foreword to this book. I think it must have been the thought of the great 'Actor Manager' ladling on the make-up (in the old days, he liked to keep it on after doing interviews) and staring into the mirror. But then we chanced upon the Leader's lavatory, and it was all that we could do to stop the notoriously scatological Rowson from taking a crap in it.

(While on the subject of mirrors, the late John Garrett once told me about his summons to go and see Tony Blair. John's reaction to hearing of the sad and untimely death of Labour leader John Smith and Tony Blair's likely accession had been, 'Well, that's me finished then,' and so it proved to be. I'll let JG take up the story: 'I went to his office and Tony Blair looked up at me, and went through all of the motions about how sorry he was that he was going to have to stand me down from the front bench. Then he said how young I looked. To which my response was: 'You should see the picture of me in the attic!' Blair looked non-plussed.')

In all I spent six years on Labour's National Executive Committee, missing a year in the middle when I was bumped off by Shahid Malik, who was later rewarded with a seat in Dewsbury before coming unstuck in the expenses scandal over wide-screen TVs, a reclining massage chair and various other ill-gotten trophies of office. He subsequently lost his seat. In some respects I am still amazed that the Blairites didn't close the NEC down altogether, despite the fact that they controlled it all of the way through. In the end it had become such a rubber stamp, and yet most of its members were unable to see the parody that they were part of. That is not to say that even a majority of the NEC members were self-interested toadies. Most were in fact the complete opposite. It's just that towing the line was the line of least resistance, and no matter how mad and bad the skirmishing between Blair, Brown and Mandelson, so long as New Labour kept winning elections, that was really all that mattered.

The Brothers (and Sisters)

THE TRADE UNIONS historically provided much of the financial support for Labour as well as crucial organisation on the ground. They had formed the Labour Representation League at the turn of the last century and refused to abandon the party when for a time in the early 1980s it seemed that almost everyone else was about to do so. The unions had been battered by the Thatcher years more than any of their leaders cared to admit. Their collective confidence was shattered – and the heavy battalions, in particular the miners and steelworkers, had been virtually obliterated. Union legislation had been enacted that outlawed secondary action, legislation that Labour – and the party's then Employment Spokesman, Tony Blair – had promised to reverse once back in power. By the time Blair was elected the unions were a shadow of their former selves: their strength lay mainly in the public sector, and their membership was maintained largely through mergers. Blair had been a sponsored Transport and General Workers' Union MP since entering Parliament in 1983, but was clearly uncomfortable amongst the working classes, when he had to give the traditional Leader's address at the joint T&G/

GMB annual reception at Labour Conference on being elected. As Shadow Employment Secretary, he had pleased them with his commitment to the Minimum Wage, but angered them when he colluded with the Tories and the employers over the closed shop. On one occasion, when he was supposed to be meeting the General Secretary of the printers' union, Tony Dubbins, Blair failed to show.

Prior to Tony's election as Leader, Lord Rothermere told me that Blair had given private assurances to Paul Dacre, editor of the *Daily Mail*, that the Thatcher anti-union legislation would not be repealed – in other words counter to much that he had publicly promised the unions. When the Durham Miners' Association invited Blair – a local MP and then leader of the party – to take the traditional salute, as had all previous Labour leaders, from Durham's famous County Hotel, Blair failed to attend. He clearly felt embarrassed by Labour's links with the unions – he thought them old-fashioned and out of place – and as his years in office stretched out, it became more and more apparent that he was not interested in restoring much of their influence.

One of the biggest complaints from the European Social Democratic parties was that Blair, through his Europe Minister Lord Simon, a former senior oil company executive, more often than not got his MEPs to side against them. By the summer of 2004, relations had almost completely broken down as Blair and Straw adamantly refused to sign up to the European Charter on Rights at Work. The new General Secretary of the TUC Brendan Barber and Blair had a ferocious argument in Number 10. Blair seemed taken aback that Barber had sworn at him over the former's support for the employers most of the time.

Blair was elected with a great deal of support from the unions but largely refused to acknowledge it. His early months in office were marked by persistent rumours that the party was set to break all ties with the unions after a hundred years. Right-wing union leaders like Sir Ken Jackson of the AEEU set about persuading Blair of their use. Although Blair had made much of the apparent ending of the block vote at conference, it survived in reduced form and the unions tried to curry favour by using their votes to support Blair at the NEC and at conference, most notably in blocking Ken Livingstone from running as Labour's candidate for Mayor of London and Rhodri Morgan running as the party's candidate for leader of the Welsh Assembly.

Occasionally the unions would make bellicose noises about the 'need to get more working-class MPs into Parliament', but more usually did the leadership's bidding in getting more clones – many of whom were pretty hostile to the unions – parachuted into safe seats.

I came across this extraordinary double standard myself, when with a colleague we decided to try and face down Gordon Brown over his Private Finance Initiative at a meeting of Labour's Economic Policy Commission in Downing Street. I pushed for a vote, as this was the only way of having something minuted and making sure that whatever we decided didn't simply disappear into a black hole. To my surprise I discovered that the Unison representative voted against our resolution, and was later informed that Dave Prentis, the union's General Secretary wasn't very happy with me, as the union had apparently decided on its 'own tactics'. Whatever these softly-softly tactics may have been, despite all the hot air over any number of years the unions never managed to dissuade Gordon from his course.

After Stephen Byers MP, a close confidant of Blair's, told four journalists in the Seafood Restaurant in Blackpool that the union link should be broken, a group of us including Kevin Maguire of the *Daily Mirror* and Martin Rowson set up the 'Seafood Group'.

We held our inaugural meeting in the same restaurant, with a number of trade unionists as our guests, and we all vowed to fight Blair and defend the union link.

The real story of the past decade was how most of the unions, even some of the left-leaning unions such as Unison, were prepared to turn a blind eye as their representatives on Labour's NEC voted against their own policies on occasion – such as over the Private Finance Initiative – a truly extraordinary accounting ruse courtesy of Gordon Brown, or rather his old chum Geoffrey Robinson, that would have got professional accountants banged up if they had come with it.

The 'four blessed Margarets' – General Secretary of the Labour Party Margaret McDonagh, Margaret Prosser of the T&G, Maggie Jones of Unison and Margaret Wall of MSF – were instrumental in shoring up Blair's position, to the detriment of their unions on the NEC, the National Policy Forum and elsewhere. Three of the Margarets were eventually sent to the House of Lords, while the fourth was rewarded with Michael Foot's old seat of Blaenau Gwent, which she promptly lost to an independent. Maggie Jones now sits in the Lords with the other Margarets, blessed to the end.

Bizarrely, some of the unions were instrumental in their own demise within the party: their votes carried through the constitutional changes that gave New Labour the power to centralise policy-making, through 'Partnership in Power'. Belatedly they came to realise that they were now junior partners – useful for their money, but not really wanted at the Blair court. When the left-winger Mick Rix was elected General Secretary of the train drivers' union ASLEF, he began to organise amongst the new breed of General Secretaries, who became in media parlance 'the awkward squad'. Rix was sufficiently dangerous for a covert action to replace him with a leader more in tune with Downing Street, and his denouement was one of the bitterest union power struggles of recent times, which finally led to the infamous 'barbecue brawl' in Hampstead and subsequently the defenestration of Rix's Blairite successor, Shaun Brady.

Almost too late the unions had realised that New Labour and Tony Blair had in some respects become hostile forces. They finally rallied at Labour's key manifesto meeting in Warwick for the National Policy Forum in July 2004. There they managed to negotiate some concessions from the Government – but Labour, once an equal partner, had almost become something of a bad employer. In the preceding months, with little fanfare and as much attention from the media, the RMT, whose Doncaster branch had first called for the setting up of the Labour Party, was expelled after it began sponsoring socialist candidates in Scotland. The firefighters – the FBU – soon followed, smarting from what they believed were the heavy-handed tactics of the government in their long-running pay dispute. With the new General Secretary of the GMB slashing back donations to Labour – and threatening to leave altogether if a third term didn't produce pro –union legislation – by the end of 2004 it began to look as though New Labour's modernisers would indeed preside over the ending of the Labour/ union link. Certainly they began to argue for more taxpayer's money for political parties, and New Labour's dependence on private donors increased. But without the unions, could there really be a Labour Party? And without the unions' bedrock support – they could still claim over seven million members – how could New Labour call on their support at election time? Increasingly it seemed that the New Labour Project had 'scorched earth' written all the way through it.

The Battle for Buckingham: Part 1

IN THE 2001 General Election I was selected as Labour's candidate in true-blue Buckingham, my home town. The powers-that-be in the party decreed that I could stand here, because I didn't have a hope in hell of winning against the Tories – then represented quite loquaciously by John Bercow. Bercow was even then in the process of moving from the uniformed wing of the Right to the soggy Blairite centre.

No one else really wanted to do it, but with agent Maggie Ewan we set about running the campaign our way. The Buckingham Labour Manifesto must have been reasonably unique as it promised amongst other things to get rid of grammar schools and re-nationalise the railways. The first was an obvious vote-loser, while the second was curiously popular in Tory commuter-land. Tony Benn and Michael Foot came to speak to a packed audience at a local church hall.

Tony Benn, while forging a path to the hall, was feted by a retired colonel washing his car. Later as we adjourned to the Market Square, local Tory councillor Sir Beville Stanier came over to greet Michael Foot, now resplendent in a multi-coloured deck chair, while two local performance artists Richard and Becky cruised the area on stilts. Sir Beville generously praised our colourful campaign.

I managed to get hold of the old Robert Maxwell-era tannoy (Maxwell was Labour MP for the area in the 1960s) and put it on the old Jag. This coincided with a visit by the *Guardian*'s Simon Hoggart, who told me that he was having some difficulty in pinning John Bercow down for an interview. 'Never mind, Simon,' said I, 'why don't you follow us around until you do?' The general madness continued as the old Jag chugged its way past Mentmore Towers (home to the Yogic flyers, who had previously stood as candidates) and onwards towards Cheddington, scene of the Great Train Robbery in 1963. I think Simon must have enjoyed his tour of the Bucks countryside, listening to the Maxwell tannoy blasting out the 'Red Flag', along with the promise to nationalise the railways. The following day he was off to Medway in Kent to spend a day with Bob Marshall-Andrews, so I was in good company.

At that time, Ken Livingstone had been banished from the Labour Party, but he and his long time adviser Simon Fletcher agreed to spend a day campaigning for me, which was good of them. I picked them up at Aylesbury Station in the Jag, which marked perhaps just the beginning of the culture shock that was to follow. 'This must be the oldest car I've ever been in,' said Ken before fastening his attention on the rural idyll that was passing us by on the other side of the A41: 'I reckon there must be more sheep than people here.'

Having been mobbed in Buckingham's market square – by at least five people – we stopped the car outside Tory campaign HQ and Livingstone picked up the old tannoy to address John Bercow, who we had reliably been informed was inside. 'Come on out, John Bercow, your time is up! Vote Labour! Vote Labour!' I wonder if

Bercow did hear the familiar nasal intonation of the people's Ken from inside his Winslow fortress, and if so what he made of it.

I tended to find Bercow an amenable man and very fair in debate – unless of course he is rattled, when the other altogether meaner John Bercow comes into play. Although the campaign began with him refusing to debate in public, he had written a harsh letter in the local press – to which my aunt, a figure of some consequence in Bercow's Conservative Association responded – telling us to speak up for what we believed in and not indulge in personal attacks.

In the later days of the campaign, my old friend Professor John Mason, the fedora-wearing Dean of Politics at Paterson University, New York, joined the campaign. Local Bucks people were clearly perplexed both by the fedora and by John's American accent urging them to 'Vote Labour' as we drove through sleepy villages. Amazingly John in the process traced his New England roots back to Buckinghamshire.

Come election day, I lost heavily – which is unsurprising in Tory Bucks – but we had managed to keep Labour in second place, ahead of the Lib Dems, so that at least was worth celebrating.

Candidate wannabe

IT WAS JANUARY 2002 and Michael Foot was in an upbeat mood. Not only had a team from Channel 4 just been around to the *Tribune* offices to interview him in connection with a documentary on Nye Bevan, he had just had a call from an old friend in Tredegar with the news that there was to be a by-election in Ogmore in South Wales. Never mind that we had just heard one of the producers ask Michael if it were true 'that Tom Driberg once gave Bevan a blow job' …

'Yes, that's right,' he insisted to me: 'You must go down there to Ogmore. They will like you there; they all know about *Tribune*.' The by-election had been caused by the death of veteran Labour MP and former whip Sir Ray Powell, a tenacious member of the 'Taffia' who had long been feared in the corridors of Westminster. In his time Sir Ray had been in charge of office space, and had kept lefties like Diane Abbott and Ken Livingstone camped out in corridors for months. Even Gordon Brown was nervous of him. I remember Sir Ray being invited to one of Brown's drinks parties in the Norman Shaw building, and Gordon being ever so solicitous with the old rascal.

Sir Ray had a reputation of running the constituency as a local fiefdom, and one of my *Tribune* colleagues Caroline Rees had reported on how everything was run from the Ogmore Labour Club and how potential members would be turned away if their faces didn't fit, by being told 'Sorry, the party is full up!' Sir Ray was sponsored by the shop workers' union USDAW, but most of the affiliated branches were 'ghost branches' which had saved him from one failed attempt to have him deselected.

Ogmore was in short a rotten borough, a former mining valley whose local economy had regressed with the passing of heavy industry. High unemployment, generational unemployment and ill health amongst an ageing population were the key local indices. Fortunately for me there were handful of left-wingers from the old *Tribune* wing of the party who had hung on in there grimly, and I went to stay with ex-Port Talbot steelworker Ron and his wife Catherine. Other local allies included my old friend Gareth Howells, who used to work for the steelworkers' union.

'Key to this constituency is Muriel Williams,' Gareth had told me. Now Muriel was the grand matriarch from these parts of the valleys, and had run the constituency for Sir Ray for many years. She had a reputation for calling a spade a spade and had recently publicly remonstrated with Tony Blair and Gordon Brown at the Wales Labour Conference, telling them to their faces to 'grow up and stop bloody arguing!'

Her mid-terrace house was on the high street of bleak ex-pit village Nantymoel, and I took one look at her and wanted to run. Muriel was a cross between Bessie Braddock and Hattie Jacques: she overflowed from her kitchen into her sparsely furnished parlour. Virtually the only decoration was an out-of-date Christmas card from Tony and Cherie. ('Someone does their homework,' thought I.) When trucks rumbled past, the windows shook.

I was motioned to sit on a rickety chair in the middle of the room, as gradually it began to fill up with members of Muriel's extended family who had all been invited to take a peek at this English boy that Michael Foot had recommended to them. It transpired that another local boy made good, Steve Morgan, a former NUS officer turned PR man, had put it about that I was married to a fabulously rich foreign lawyer, so suspicions were further heightened.

'So what makes you think that you can *possibly* follow in the footsteps of Sir Ray, who as you know was a giant of a man?' Before I could even muster a flabby response, Muriel continued: 'Did you know that he died with his teacup in his hand?' I confessed that I was unaware of this detail – although it was later recounted to me that Sir Ray had indeed been found lying prostrate in his Dolphin Square flat, teacup in hand.

Multiple pairs of eyes watched my every reaction, silently registering I do not know what. The tension was broken when one of the family members answered the phone and said, 'Muriel, Steve Morgan for you!' To which she responded, 'I'm not talking to him!' This I took as a vague sign of hope – fleeting, as it happened.

Despite its weather-beaten appearance, Ogmore was full of characters. On one occasion Ron said, 'You must come and meet the branch secretary, Dai Glum.'

'Why is he called that?', I asked.

'Because he's never very happy.'

And then there was another local member, Dai 'Two Lamps'. 'Well, it was in the war see, and Dai was on his motorbike. He was driving along, like, and he sees two headlamps heading towards him. So Dai thinks, "I better get between those two bikes." But it was an army lorry, see.'

I went to see the agent with my wife Yasmin in tow. 'You'll have to move here if you get selected,' he said. But on that particular day I wasn't in the best of moods. Another member told me that he had it on 'good authority' that the selection panel presided over by Charles Clarke – then the appointed party chairman – would block me. I immediately phoned Clarke, who categorically denied it.

As I was to learn later, the party machine had decided that a university lecturer named Huw Irranca Davies was going to be the candidate. I remember talking with Sir Russell Goodway (leader of South Glamorgan County Council), who was also seeking nomination, and whom I knew well. He had told me of the extraordinary odds at a Swansea betting shop for Davies – who at that stage no one knew had even declared an interest.

This whole episode left me feeling quite sick. Clarke had clearly misled me. It wasn't enough that he had beaten me in Norwich at a previous selection; he had done me in again.

I was so infuriated by the way in which I and my local supporters had been treated that I penned the following article for the *Independent* based on my experience at the time:

'Ogmore? Where is Ogmore?', asked the young BBC researcher. What lies beyond Offa's Dyke may have been something of a mystery to her, but a by-election was shortly to take place in one of Labour's safest seats in South Wales.

So here were some of the spicy ingredients that have gone in to making the Ogmore Labour Party Welsh cawl – or broth. I hope that the party's new standard-bearer in the constituency has an appetite for it, or better still, pours the stinking broth down the sink. (That candidate is not me – I was excluded from the party's shortlist at the eleventh hour.)

Ogmore, which comprises three former mining valleys in south-west Wales, has been Labour for as long as anyone can remember.

Locals claim that the last proper canvass of voters took place shortly after the General Strike in 1926, when the Communist Party posed something of a threat. The area suffers multiple social deprivation, the top end of the valleys are now probably poorer than they were twenty years ago.

Local Labour Party members – truly some of the most long-suffering people that it is possible to imagine – know the ingredients. They wouldn't recommend it to anyone. For Ogmore is often thought of as a rotten borough, presided over by two warring clans for more than two decades.

In one corner are the supporters of the late MP, Sir Ray Powell, including members of his extended family. At one time around a dozen 'Powellistas' had positions of one kind or another in the local Labour Party. Unkind souls have likened the clan to the Kim Il Sung dynasty in North Korea.

In the other corner, looming menacingly, is the leader of one of the local authorities in the area, Councillor Jeff Jones. This splenetic figure drives the Wales Labour Party to distraction, and while his targets are not always misplaced, personal animosities are so entrenched and bitter as to make the 1984-5 miners' strike a tea party.

Councillor Jones has now transferred his hostilities to Sir Ray's chosen successor, the capable and ambitious Mayor of Cardiff, Russell Goodway. Locals fear a bloodbath – or the near imminent expulsion from the party of Councillor Jones, for his attacks on Mr Goodway.

Some of those who preside over the Ogmore selection do not like new members of the Labour Party either. They would prefer them to stay away. One young woman took a day off during the general election and offered to help the party she had recently joined. 'Not needed today,' was the brusque reply.

Other veterans recall the moribund trade union branches that were once mustered to save Sir Ray from being deselected. Others laugh wearily as they recall the ancient, but revered practice of 'signing up dead members' in order to preserve near defunct branches. Folk memory, once tapped, produces a line of one-liners designed to cheer the old Soviet politburo. My favourites are, 'Don't you know, comrade that democracy means to conform?' Or this: 'Comrade. Sometimes democracy can go too far!'

On Tuesday evening, as one local Labour branch finally wearied of the Powell dynasty and voted to deselect his daughter, the local Wales Assembly member, another branch gathered to vote a few miles down the road. 'This is a secret ballot,' a member was told. 'But you have to write down your names at the bottom of the ballot paper.'

'South Wales radicalism?', said an MP from an adjoining constituency: 'It's a myth!' One of the questions to Labour hopefuls from the party's selection panel on Monday night in Cardiff was: 'How to do you propose to interest young people in the Labour Party and politics?' How indeed, when a combination of old right-wing Labour machine politics and New Labour control-freakery have produced an all-embracing hybrid which snuffs out most signs of political life?

In retrospect I was naive to imagine that it might be possible to gather enough support from local members to win the Labour nomination, without being scrubbed out by machine politicians in the Spartan surroundings of a committee room in Transport House, Cardiff.

The man that Tony Blair made chairman of the Labour Party, Charles Clarke, announced to colleagues and the press that my performance in front of the panel was 'very poor' and that this was the reason for the banning order. As a result I would not be able to go and make my case to the long-suffering members of the Ogmore Labour Party at the final selection meeting.

The real reason I suspect was that I had answered Clarke's questions in a way that was unacceptable to Labour's ruling cabal. On the recent attacks launched in Afghanistan, I said that I thought going to war in that country would be a huge mistake, and we shouldn't be dragged into it. I also said that I remained opposed to Gordon Brown's 'Public Private Finance Initiative', because were storing up huge costs for the future.

In fact the tom-tom drums in the valleys had been drumming out a distinct message almost immediately that I had thrown my hat into the Ogmore cawl. I had cause to telephone Charles Clarke to tell him that a leading councillor was telling members 'not to bother with Seddon because he won't be on the short-list'.

Neil Kinnock – once a valleys firebrand, now a European Commissioner – has been backing long-serving assistant Jan Royall for the nomination in Ogmore. Others reported that one candidate had been told by a senior government minister: 'We want a safe pair of hands who is 100 per cent New Labour.'

Naively, I believed that being a member of Labour's National Executive Committee and the party's candidate selection committee would deter any outbreak of control-freakery. Had not the Rhodri Morgan and Ken Livingstone debacles brought an end to the culture of the political fix? I did not reckon on another stock-in phrase, namely that I had 'no local connections'. In other words, I was not Welsh. Hilariously, a couple of days later, I received an invitation from an official of Plaid Cymru to join them.

Ogmore – and other areas that are similar to it that have been treated as private fiefdoms – deserve better from Labour. The party's new standard bearer in the constituency will need a good deal of luck and fortitude if the old mould is to be broken.

Pinky and Perky –
Meet Tony and Gordon!

NEWLY ENSCONCED AS editor of *Tribune* in summer 1993 in the peeling offices of the old Transport and General Workers' Union in Gray's Inn Road, Kings Cross, London, there were at least two traditional 'meet and greets' for me. The first of course was with Tony Benn, whom I had first met as a seventeen-year-old schoolboy protesting against Tory cuts in 1978 in Wiltshire; the second with Arthur Scargill.

I knocked on Benn's door in Notting Hill, and a basement window flew open. Tony Benn's head appeared, pipe firmly clenched: 'You'll have to come in this way,' he pointed. Once inside the Benn basement, I asked him about the tramp who had made the shed in his front garden home for a while. 'Yesh, well Caroline used to take things to him. He was quite a lonely soul you know.' Tony's basement was cluttered, to put it mildly. Pieces of paper were stuck everywhere, even hanging from the ceiling. 'Now I want you to listen to this,' said Tony as he put an old record on a turntable. And so it was that I drank a mug of tea with Tony Benn while listening to a scratchy budget speech by Sir Stafford Cripps.

Because as everyone should know, Cripps was one of *Tribune*'s founders – and benefactors.

Years later, my old Jaguar overheated in Notting Hill outside Tony's house. As I was staring forlornly at the steam geyser shooting up from under the bonnet, a familiar figure hove into view. 'You need some fresh water for that, comrade!', said Tony Benn as he sailed past.

'You'll be asked to go and see Tony Blair next!' joked someone. Come to think of it, I had already, back in 1992 when I'd organised a lobbying meeting of North-East MPs, including Tony Blair, with what was then the National Coal Board in Victoria, headed up by one Neil Clark. I recalled meeting Blair for the first time – back then most of the North-East MPs were ex-union officials or former industrial workers. I remember him being charming and personable, and also that the Chairman of the Coal Board must have been quite taken with him, as I overheard him asking Tony if he would like to go for lunch one day – which is more than he had offered to the other MPs and ex-miners present like John Cummings and Billy Etherington.

And then came a call, one desultory day in the *Tribune* offices. 'It's Anji Hunter from Tony Blair's office', said Sheila Noble, the veteran production manager who had helped keep the *Tribune* show on the road for nearly thirty years. It transpired that Tony was keen to meet me, since I had just been made editor, and at his house in Islington, North London. He came to the door when I knocked, dressed in casual trousers and a pullover. I assumed the woman by his side was his wife so I said, 'Hi, Cherie!', but Tony said that she was his housekeeper. Once inside, he made a couple of mugs of coffee and we went to his study. Given his already well-known impatience with the traditional Labour Party, I was surprised to see on his bookshelves a copy of a book entitled *A*

History of the Lancashire Area NUM, but thought better to ask about it. There then followed a fairly anodyne romp through, and cull of, Labour shibboleths. Tony thought that public ownership was old-fashioned, to which I said, 'What about Caledonian MacBrayne?' This was the Scottish ferry company which kept – as a public service – the Western Isles supplied and connected. He said that people in his Sedgefield constituency wanted to be middle-class, and that not everyone wanted to sit in rows in working men's clubs. Was Tony thinking of Bernard Manning's Embassy Club? At which point I managed to spill some of my coffee, while Tony selflessly poured some from his brimming cup into mine.

Interestingly though, he was quite enthusiastic about John Prescott. Even then Blair was canny enough to see how Prescott could be the northern foil for his planned sacking of the Labour monastery. 'Peter [Mandelson] doesn't think much of him,' said Tony, 'but you know, I do!'

So what to make of the man everyone seemed to think was Labour's rising young star? He was so very different from any Labour figure I had met. There was a lightness of touch, an easy approachability. Blair was very much the protean, but also curiously square and hardly the radical that half the commentariat had him out to be. His reflex actions were automatically of the right.

Max Hastings recalls taking Blair out to lunch at White's Club around about that time and the fact that Blair was more than happy to settle for the least expensive food and wine. He wasn't showy or greedy. I remember leaving Blair and liking him. But I also recall having lunch with the late Hugo Young of the *Guardian* in Gray's Inn Road shortly afterwards. I said that I thought that Blair was a 'lightweight', a view not shared by Young – who shortly afterwards cited 'urgent business to attend to' and left without even offering to pay his share of the bill.

My early take on Blair which emerged in *Tribune* was later commented on by the writer and novelist, Frederick Forsyth, who a year or so into Blair's subsequent leadership of the Labour Party wrote that 'only two people, Mark Seddon of *Tribune* and to an extent from the other end of the spectrum, Charles Moore [then editor of the *Daily Telegraph*] refused to go along with the Blair media love-in'.

That first meeting with Blair must have been deemed a success, because two weeks later another invitation came, this time to meet Tony in the Commons. I was late, and as I got out of the lift I spotted two young researchers, James Purnell and Ed Richards, playing fake cricket in the corridor. On closer inspection, both appeared to be wearing some sort of black eyeliner. I knew Ed Richards, because he had worked for one of the postal unions, and he along with Neal Lawson were part of a group of young people who were soon come to become known as 'modernisers'. I liked Ed, despite the fact that he once tried to rewrite an interview I had conducted with Gordon Brown, and seemed very keen that *Tribune*'s veteran lobby correspondent Hugh MacPherson should be quietly 'retired'.

MacPherson was a highly respected journalist who had been an active Bevanite at Glasgow University, and whose time in the Labour Club there was shared with John Smith and Donald Dewar, who had been Gaitskellites. Michael Foot had given MacPherson *Tribune*'s lobby pass, and the latter wrote for free for *Tribune*, earning his living editing the liberal-minded John Lewis in-house communications magazine. But MacPherson had already crossed swords with Labour's young Employment Spokesman, and reported in *Tribune* on Blair's ability to weave his way around issues of principle. 'He's like a political blancmange,' said Hugh. MacPherson wasn't particularly enamoured of Gordon Brown either, and it was to Brown that Ed Richards answered. The occasional story began to emerge in the press about MacPherson, namely that he was a wealthy man who worked for a big company in the city. Clearly the idea was to diminish him in the eyes of left-wingers.

'We don't except to change *Tribune*,' Tony told me at that second meeting, 'all we ask is to be allowed to have our say as well' – which seemed fairly reasonable to me. The briefings against MacPherson and the suggestions to me that I should take his lobby card, I suspect originated from Gordon Brown's people.

Another early indication of how Brown could move hard and fast to remove opponents came shortly afterwards with the annual election to the *Tribune* Group of Labour MPs. The *Tribune* Group had risen from the ashes of the Bevanite 'Keep Left' group, and as its name suggests acted as a supporters' group within the Parliamentary Labour Party. The Group didn't really have the influence that it once had, and was seen increasingly as a 'soft Left' grouping, with the Socialist Campaign Group to its left. But more recently a couple of soft Left radical MPs, Peter Hain and Roger Berry, had revived the Tribune Group, and in particular were critical of what they saw as Gordon Brown's increasingly cautious economic policy. Hain and Berry argued for a more interventionist, Keynesian approach, and for their sins were toppled from their positions within the *Tribune* Group. I was having a drink with Newcastle MP and staunch Gordon Brown supporter Nick Brown in the bar that was once known as 'The Kremlin' when the Hain/Berry defenestration took place. Gordon, with the help of Nick Brown I suspect, had organised a group of distinctly non-Tribunite MPs to go and join the group – and boot

Hain and Berry out. This whole episode marked the beginning of the end for the group, which from then on became thoroughly on-message, renamed itself subsequently the 'New Tribune Group', and then finally became a 'virtual reality' grouplet before disappearing for good.

Gordon Brown was of course Labour's Scottish tribal chief. A deeply serious political figure, he was the perfect antidote to Tony Blair, the political lightweight. John Smith expected him to follow in his footsteps, as did most of the power brokers in the Labour Party. But no one thought that Smith's tenure would be so short. John Smith had gone out of his way to reconnect with all sections of the Labour Party, including with *Tribune*, and I still have a letter from him saying that he would be very keen for *Tribune* and its readers to take a full part in the policy review process that was taking place in the aftermath of John Major's victory over Neil Kinnock in 1992.

I was on holiday in Tobermory on the Isle of Mull – ironically, Smith is buried on Iona, just off the coast of Mull – when one of my friends came back from the newsagent with the news that Smith had died of a heart attack. This came as a real shock, not because Smith was a great populist, but because he was so transparently a decent man. Sitting in our rented cottage, all of us came to the early conclusion that Blair, not Brown, would be the next leader of the Labour Party – not something we were enthusiastic about at all.

I had gone to work for Brown during the 1992 General Election, along with Neal Lawson, Ed Richards and Delyth Evans, with PR guru Barry Delaney frequently popping by to offer advice. The Brown office was not based at the then Labour headquarters, but in an office near the Elephant and Castle in South London. As I was a regular writer for *Tribune* – I had yet to become editor

– I was the only journalist on the team, and as such went along to the Conservative election campaign press conferences and attempted to throw in questions drawn up by Brown and his team. Occasionally John Smith would drop in, but by and large the Brown team ploughed its own furrow. Towards the end of the campaign – one in which I had the distinct impression that Brown knew that Labour was going to lose – he took us out for a morose dinner. I recall asking him what he through the worst thing Margaret Thatcher had done during her years in power. Brown replied that it was the Tory policy of making poor people in his Scottish constituency take out loans for essentials, such as cookers or heaters. I still have the present he gave me for my work for the campaign: a biography of Margaret Thatcher by Hugo Young, which struck me as strange then as it still does now. It was signed, after a fashion, by what looked like a stamped signature.

Any visitor to the Brown or Blair offices during those early days in opposition would have been struck, as was I, as to how close the two men were – and that Peter Mandelson was never far away either. There were lots of yellow Post-it notes in both Blair and Brown's offices reading 'Peter called' or 'Please call Peter'. All three had become increasingly impatient with what they viewed as the slow pace of 'reform' under Smith, although Brown was seen as the most loyal of the three. Any remaining serious threat to the rise of the 'Labour modernisers' had probably gone with the departure of former Labour Shadow Cabinet member and representative of the thinking soft Left, Bryan Gould, to become an academic in his native New Zealand. Gould, I suspect, had calculated that the tide was running inexorably in the modernisers' favour.

I remember on one occasion going to interview Brown for *Tribune* and arriving at his office in the Norman Shaw building in Westminster. Gordon said that we would have to keep it tight as he would be 'going over to Prime Minister's Questions with Tony.' But when the appointed hour arrived, a spotty youth put his head around the corner – perhaps it was Blair's researcher Tim Allan, who became the model for Martin Rowson's 'Blair's Babes' cartoon strip in *Tribune*, in which Allan and chums were depicted in nappies.

Allan, or whoever it was said: 'Sorry Gordon, but Tony has already gone over.' At which point Gordon Brown's face contorted and turned ashen. He flung a pencil down on the table with such force that it took off and ricocheted around the room. There then followed a period of intense silence. Clearly this wasn't a relationship made in heaven. Subsequently, *Observer* columnist Andrew Rawnsley reported on a whole series of incidents involving Brown losing his temper, amidst allegations of 'bullying'. Knowing Brown, I suspect that he was mortified to read all of this. The truth is that despite his failings in recognising the enormous loyalty shown to him by some, he retained the loyal service of key staff members for many years. Frankly, I find the idea that Brown is a 'bully' quite ridiculous. That he came to rely on the services of some who could bully and rant is not in doubt. My own theory, for what it is worth, is that Brown set far greater store to his relationship with Blair than Blair did with him. As the scales fell from Brown's eyes, and he found himself being briefed against, probably largely by Blair's main ally Peter Mandelson, he decided to surround himself with people like Charlie Whelan, who could give as good as they got.

Brown's relationship with Mandelson was even more turbulent than with Blair. Since much of the Labour Party didn't like Mandelson much either, Brown would sometimes make great play of the animosity between them. On one occasion he came to speak to a *Tribune* fundraiser on the South Bank, and raised the roof with a joke presumably penned for him by John O'Farrell, who normally wasn't all that funny. 'Peter Mandelson asked if he could borrow 10p to phone a friend,' said a deadpan Gordon. 'I gave him 20p and said, "Phone all of them!"' Martin Rowson claims that he went up to Gordon afterwards and said, 'Gordon, that was a truly terrible speech.' Given that Martin is as honest as the day is long, I don't doubt him, but in Brown's defence I had seen that his hand-written speech – in blue felt tip – had been caught up in the deluge that had opened up just before the event began. Gordon's eyesight wasn't good anyway, and that he was able to make anything of the vast blue smudged paper disintegrating in his hands, was really quite something.

The Blair-Brown relationship was the all-consuming media obsession for much of a decade. Sections of the Left and the trade unions tended to shelter under the umbrella of the brooding Chancellor, partly because he knew our language but also because although in essence he was signed up to a neo-liberal economic world view, he did genuinely believe that there was still room in the system to help the worst off. In this he didn't disappoint, and many of the micro-measures people came to associate with the government or the stealth taxes can be laid at his door. Brown was a political giant, with an intellect that far outshone that of the great 'actor manager' Tony Blair, but Brown was never the consummate media performer, and despite his private warmth and good nature never really came over well on the doorstep, except perhaps in his native Scotland, where they did understand him better.

In 1995 I decided to run for election to Labour's ruling National Executive Committee, as the rules had been changed to allow ordinary members to replace MPs in the constituency section. The rules had been changed in order to keep out MPs such as Diane Abbott and Ken Livingstone (who had famously beaten Peter

Mandelson) and ensure that the new constituency section would be the rubbers-stamp of the Blairites and Party General Secretary Margaret McDonagh, who with the passage of time I came to quite like.

Gordon Brown had me into his office, and told me I was pleased I was running (the Blairites weren't), but that I should be careful of allying myself with 'Trots'. Since our slate of Left candidates was being marshalled by a former member of the establishment-leaning 'Labour Solidarity', Tim Pendry, and since none of my co-conspirators could remotely be described as 'Trots', I wasn't altogether sure what Gordon meant. However, he did say that if I didn't rock the boat too much I should eventually land myself a safe Labour seat.

In the meantime I was to serve on the party's Economic Policy Commission, which was supposed to meet monthly, and was chaired by Gordon Brown. The meetings continued when Labour was in government, although with less regularity. On one occasion I turned up at 11 Downing Street and was ushered through to a meeting room. Looking around the room, I couldn't help but notice that all of the regular faces seem to have been replaced. Was this another New Labour purge? And if it was, how had I survived? I asked the guy next to me when he had joined the Policy Commission. 'What commission? We are the diplomatic mission of Algeria.' I had got the wrong date.

Inside Downing Street with Rupert Murdoch

DURING THE MID-1990s the Blairites were putting a good deal of energy into ensuring that in future the party conference and NEC would have significantly less power over a future Labour government. Without a trace of irony, this was all part and parcel of 'Partnership in Power', and the key to getting the affiliated unions to accept it was Jon Cruddas, who was then part of Tony Blair's Downing Street Policy Unit.

Cruddas had taken to having meetings with *Tribune*'s then deputy editor John Blevin. John and Jon would meet in odd places and hide behind pillars in a dance of weird deception. Blevin was a refugee from the Communist daily the *Morning Star*, and John Cryer, also an ex-*Morning Star* staffer, had been particularly persuasive in getting John Blevin in. I liked him – he was a Scouser with a cracking sense of humour who had once worked in the Liverpool Parks Department – but it was quite clear to me why he was taken with all of this 'Partnership in Power' nonsense, for the script might as well have been lifted from the old CP Central Committee.

Perhaps out of desperation, Jon Cruddas invited me round to 10 Downing Street to discuss the changes and see if *Tribune* would support them. On arriving at his office, I spotted Tony Blair's long-time adviser Anji Hunter walking down the corridor arm-in-arm with a grizzled, familiar figure. It was Rupert Murdoch. Now I had heard rumours that Murdoch was a frequent visitor to Downing Street and of course we already knew that both Blair and his press spokesman Alastair Campbell had flown across the world to meet Murdoch and his executives at Hayling Island, Australia, at the Dirty Digger's expense, before Blair had become Prime Minister. Shortly afterwards, Labour's longstanding policy of restricting media cross-ownership was dropped in order to allow Murdoch to further extend his media reach once Blair was in government. And shortly afterwards, Murdoch's British newspapers began shifting their allegiance to Tony Blair, and the *Sun* came out in support of Blair in the 1997 General Election. I had been tipped off from the inside, and called the then editor Stuart Higgins and asked him if it might be true, several hours before the presses ran. 'I categorically deny it!', Higgins had said.

Still, it was something of a shock to see Murdoch in the flesh, so obviously being schmoozed. The media mogul had long been one of our targets at *Tribune*, since I had strong memories of how he went about firing 5,000 printers when he moved his plant to Wapping, as I'd spent some time on the picket lines with them. But more than that, the culture of 'Murdochracy' had infected everything. The Dirty Digger always got what he wanted.

On spotting Murdoch in Downing Street I was immediately sworn to secrecy by Cruddas – and managed to keep quiet at least until the following day, when I turned up for my weekly shift on the 'Londoner's Diary' at the *Evening Standard*. After all that Murdoch and his newspapers had done to destroy the Labour Party

under Michael Foot and Neil Kinnock, and their more successful destruction of the Fleet Street print unions, it seemed outrageous that Blair and his people were going out of their way to suck up to him and some of his editors. Blair and Campbell seemed incapable of understanding that Murdoch's papers were followers of fashion, and that the tide was flowing in Labour's favour. The idea that the *Sun* would reprise the 1992 eve-of-election, 'If Kinnock wins today will the last person to leave Britain please turn out the lights', with Neil Kinnock depicted as a light bulb, was frankly risible.

Writing in *Tribune*, former editor turned MP Chris Mullin advised Blair to make Murdoch his first priority upon reaching Downing Street. 'Hit hard and hit fast,' wrote Mullin. Some hope. Blair, Campbell and their entourage spent the next decade cosying up to Murdoch and giving him whatever he wanted, a practice that was to be continued under David Cameron's government. If there was a reception in Downing Street, you could guarantee that Rebekah Brooks – editor of the *News of the World* and *Sun* before becoming chief executive of Murdoch's News International – would be there. Murdoch in turn continued to lower the benchmark of tabloid journalism, using the *Sun* and *News of the World* in particular as a battering ram of menace and supposition. Despite widespread collusion between his titles and the police, it was later to be revealed that some of his journalists routinely bugged their way inside the mobile phones of celebrities and politicians. Fortunately for the establishment, Murdoch's papers were so debased that they didn't go for the inside dope on how for instance a small number of bankers had virtually brought down the whole edifice of Anglo-American capitalism. No, they were only interested in trawling for celebrity trivia – and messages from the mobile phones of dead school children.

In 2001 Rebekah Wade, as she then was, famously ran a nauseating campaign to identify names and addresses of suspected paedophiles, which famously led to a paediatrician being attacked in Newport. At the Labour Party Conference I had spotted her in the bar of the Metropole Hotel, sporting a ghoulish badge featuring murdered schoolgirl Sarah Payne, in whose name the campaign for 'Sarah's Law' was being waged. (John Prescott had made a plonker of himself when telling the BBC that Wade's *News of the World* campaign was 'public-spirited' – unlike the less public-spirited hacking into of JP's mobile phone of course.)

As Wade made her way out of the hotel, I went up and told her that she was running a squalid little campaign, and that I would be publishing a picture of her, complete with her address, on the front cover of *Tribune* under the headline 'Rebekah Wade – We Know Where You Live!'

I did so – and subsequently heard that she had had a copy of that front page framed and hung on her office wall.

I suspect that, in return, Rebekah had someone find out where I live – so I am looking forward to contacting New Scotland Yard to find out what else News International may have known about me.

On the Downing Street sofa with Tony

TONY BLAIR FAMOUSLY ran much of his government from a sofa in 10 Downing Street, where key decisions were taken without civil servants being present and notes being taken. Successive Cabinets allowed themselves to be turned into echo chambers, meekly going along with Gordon Brown's iron grip over economic policy and Blair's all-too-frequent puerile homilies. You only have to read a few pages of Alastair Campbell's diaries to realise just how shallow the thought and speech processes were for the daily business of opposition and then government. This was usually the case at Labour's NEC as well, although there was a core of us who rebelled and voted against the line. In the Shadow Cabinet and then the Cabinet the 'democratic centralism' of New Labour pervaded, broken substantially only when Robin Cook resigned on the eve of the Iraq war.

In my early days as a member of Labour's NEC and editor of *Tribune* I would occasionally be asked round to sit on the sofa to have a chat with Tony. On one occasion I recall being thus invited after the NEC had steamrollered through new rules to effectively block Ken Livingstone from being Labour's first mayoral candidate for London. I had kicked up quite a fuss about this as it was all such a transparent, self-defeating fix. I couldn't understand how it was that more seasoned politicos than me could make such a mess of things, especially as Livingstone was so obviously going to be the choice of the London Labour Party and was popular amongst Londoners. Everyone told me that I might as well tell Tony what I thought and take two key issues in with me, rather than a whole shopping list. So I began by telling Tony that I thought Barbara Castle was right and that we should restore the State Earnings Related Pensions. Blair seemed to be sympathetic , but said that the problem there was that Gordon Brown wouldn't budge. As for Ken Livingstone, Blair seemed curiously non-committal. In fact he seemed to be more interested in hearing why people like me thought he should be allowed to run and why he would make for a good Mayor – presumably in order for Tony to do him in even more comprehensively. Tony and Ken, oddly enough, were quite similar creatures. Ken, of course, was probably the only left-winger really ever to beat Blair at his own game. Needless to say, he ended up being booted out of the Labour Party, running as an independent in London and winning handsomely.

Michael Foot's approaching ninetieth birthday was something even New Labour couldn't ignore – although to be fair to Tony Blair he always went out of his way to say nice things about Michael, even though the subtext was that most of what Michael and a good section of the Labour Party had always stood for should be confined to the darker recesses of the attic.

The idea was to hold a birthday party in the garden of 10 Downing Street, but the next problem was how to get Michael there. Enter Mick Rix, General Secretary of the train drivers' union, in whose magnificent Hampstead mansion, once owned by the Beecham family, *Tribune* was then based. (That *Tribune* ended up in such palatial surroundings in the first place was very much down to Mick, who promised to 'sort something out' for us over a lunch in the Gay Hussar. The building itself featured a giant green marble ball on the balustrade heading up the stairs, which was supposed to represent a Beecham's Pill. Under Mick Rix's highly enlightened leadership of ASLEF, the building would come alive. There was nothing strange in looking out into the garden and seeing the actor Richard Wilson going through his paces with some young thespians, as a Hampstead orchestra tuned up in one of the rooms downstairs. There was an ASLEF gay, bisexual and transgender branch that would sometimes turn up, one of whose members served in a depot in Barnsley. (Sadly it all seemed to go a bit downhill after the Mick Rix era. The union recently demanded that a cartoon collection loaned by Bill Hagerty be got rid of 'because there weren't any trains in any of the pictures', and took great delight in threatening to chuck *Tribune* out onto the streets, as the union's greatest asset, replete with so much of its heritage, was sold off.)

With Michael's party imminent, Mick called up in high dudgeon. 'I bow to no one in my admiration for Michael,' he fumed, 'but I'm not a bloody chauffeur!' It transpired that some underling from 10 Downing Street had called up and asked if Mick would drive Michael to Downing Street. I had been having mixed feelings about the event, especially if Michael was going to be patronised or a bunch of the Shadow Cabinet would be there pretending to be lefties for the afternoon. But Michael's friend Jenny Stringer had other ideas. 'You've got your car haven't you? Can you take Michael?'

We approached the gates of Downing Street in my battered Mercedes, and once clear I drove up to the front door, whereupon

Tony Blair emerged – and did a double take: not only, I suspect, at the state of my car, and perhaps the Chairman Mao pennant I had hanging from the mirror (a cab driver had given me it in Beijing), but also because it was me that emerged from the driver's seat, and not Mick Rix. He soon recovered his composure and helped guide Michael through to what he euphemistically called 'the Rose Garden', a particularly silly steal of a concept from the White House. I remember bumping into Bruce Kent, who had also been invited, and who was threatening to perform a 'citizen's arrest' on Blair for 'war crimes'. But somehow Bruce had lost his nerve or was enjoying the convivial Old Labour company and the summer warmth too much. The much-talked-about 'citizen's arrest' of Tony Blair in his back garden didn't take place. The Old Labour battalion, including Jack Jones, respectfully listened to Tony Blair warbling on, clapped politely, and then shuffled off.

There was no putsch.

On Peter Mandelson

SELF-SERVING, EGOTISTICAL AND narcissistic. These epithets accurately describe the personality of former Business Secretary, former Northern Ireland Secretary and former Industry Secretary, Lord Peter Mandelson. But even now, stretching out from the political grave, Lord Mandelson, leaning on the crutch that is his overblown autobiography *The Third Man,* revealed that he wants one day to return to frontline politics! To which, I hope that all good people say in unison, 'Not over our dead bodies!'

Peter Mandelson rejoices in the breathless prose of all too many commentators who fed from his hand and who lauded him as the 'architect of New Labour', and that so significant was his role during the Blair-Brown years that he must be counted as one of their equals – hence the title to his book.

He is not in the same league as Blair, still less Brown. But if he wants to be remembered as the architect of that weird sect New Labour, a star-struck fan club that was run with the same élan as the old East German Communist Party, let him. Even now the *Guardian* talks of him 'saving his beloved Labour Party.' Excuse me from intruding into this love-in, but the last time I looked, Labour had lost five million voters during Mandelson's New Labour era, the party is emptied of members, and it is broke. To cap it all, in 2010 it had its worst General Election result since 1983 – although the *Guardian* newspaper's support for Nick Clegg's Lib Dems at the election can't have helped. 'New Labour', in case Mandelson and his friends hadn't noticed, became a term of abuse some time ago.

However, in claiming this dubious honour, Mandelson would also like to be remembered as the architect of Labour's historic 1997 landslide – a myth recalibrated *ad nauseam* by his friends in the media. Well, Joe Haines, the former street-fighting adjutant to Harold Wilson – no shrinking violet, he – offered up this analysis in a review for *Tribune* of another recently released book, *The Alastair Campbell Diaries*: 'an anthology of hate, obsession, spin and rampant ambition.'

Haines declares how 'We won in 1997 not because of their brilliance [Mandelson, Campbell, Blair *et al*] but because the nation was irretrievably fed up with John Major, and he couldn't have won a raffle in which he bought all the tickets.'

I first met Peter Mandelson in 1993 at a drinks party organised by Gordon Brown in the Commons. Back then, Mandelson was followed around by a gauche young researcher by the name of Derek Draper. Draper, nicknamed 'Mutley' (and later 'Dolly'), told me that he had bought Peter some pink handcuffs for his birthday, which was thoughtful of him. Both Draper and Mandelson seemed very keen to denigrate John Smith, the then Labour leader, which they did in a malevolent, snide fashion – the sort of behaviour that sadly came to epitomise so much of the nastiness of the New Labour years to come. I reached some early conclusions about Peter Mandelson back then and in the years since he has never failed to disappoint.

Lest we forget, as plain Peter Mandelson he lasted barely five months as Secretary of State for Industry, having been forced to resign for failing to declare a £373,000 home loan from his pal Geoffrey Robinson MP. Having militated against the much-loved Mo Mowlam, he persuaded Blair to let him have her job as Northern Ireland Secretary, this time lasting barely a year before he was accused of helping arrange a British passport for Indian billionaire Srichard Hinduja, something for which he was later cleared. Mr Hinduja, it will be recalled, had promised a cool £1 million for Mandelson's beloved Millennium Dome, a ludicrous white elephant that finally did for any notion of 'Cool Britannia'. Bizarrely, although Mandelson bleats in *The Third Man* that he 'fought for ten years to make the relationship of Blair and Brown work in government', Gordon Brown rehabilitated the man who had caused him so much grief over the years and made him Business Secretary – presumably on the basis that having him inside the tent would lance some of Mandelson's legendary poison.

Mandelson talks of his 'intense' relations with the two men, something that used to have the late Leo Abse speculating that the real story of New Labour was one of unrequited love. But is anyone really interested? Does anyone really care any more? And why did the Labour Party have to be effectively closed down, ostensibly to avoid division, when those at the top were responsible for more divisive activities than a whole row of Derek Hattons?

Mandelson told us magisterially that he would not be endorsing any of the 2010 Labour leadership contestants – because he is a past master at secretly backing one while pretending to support all of the others. He didn't publicly back Tony Blair when he stood for the Labour leadership either, for exactly the same reasons: instead he operated under the pseudonym 'Bobby'. When shortly after John Smith's death we attempted to reveal his covert role in *Tribune*, Mo Mowlam called me, having been assured by Blair that Mandelson was not involved in the campaign, to threaten legal action if we went ahead and published the story. Why the threatened heavy hand? Because Mandelson was so unpopular amongst Labour MPs that Blair's leadership hopes would have been doomed if the MPs got to know.

Don't get me wrong. I can see that Lord Mandelson is as a capable as he is intelligent. Had he not allowed himself to be sucked into the world of the *nouveau riche* – Nat Rothschild, Russian oligarchs and the superficiality afforded by them – he could have concentrated on being a good government minister. Had he been shorter on spinning and plotting and longer on philosophy and empathy, he could have become a successful and even long serving British Foreign Secretary.

But now it is all over for Peter Mandelson, in British Labour politics at least. Clement Attlee once famously said to the disputatious Harold Laski that 'a period of silence from you would be welcome', which is more or less what any of the Labour contenders for the leadership would have wanted from Mandelson.

Farewell to Footie!

I WAS DUE to go and visit Michael Foot at his home in Hampstead on the Wednesday afternoon, but then the sad, but not entirely unexpected news broke of his passing at the grand old age of ninety-six.

I first met Foot in 1983, as he led the 'People's March for Jobs' contingent into Norwich, where he delivered a stunning piece of pre-election oratory. I still have a photograph of a laughing Michael standing next to his old friend Spike Milligan, champagne glass in hand. Underneath, Spike has written: 'We'll win the election, I promise!'

Lazy, shorthand journalism will make much of that unhappy, strife-ridden interlude of the early 1980s for Foot and his beloved wife Jill Craigie, but the Labour party would have disintegrated without him at the time. Better and more inspiring to look at the most extraordinary achievements of this man, who walked with the greats and, for a while, was arguably the greatest living Englishman.

Foot will always be associated with *Tribune* – his first cub reporter's story from the bitter post-general strike Harworth

Colliery dispute was written there, and his long association with the *Tribune* greats Aneurin Bevan, Barbara Castle and William Mellor began. Foot was editor of *Tribune* twice, and at a time when the British establishment sought appeasement with Nazi Germany, Foot's *Tribune* was first to bellow, 'Hitler means war!' But then, this was the weekly that championed the International Brigades in Spain and denounced Rothermere's *Daily Mail* and its sympathies for Oswald Mosley (expressed in that seminal headline 'Hurrah for the Blackshirts!').

If *Tribune* was for fighting fascism, there was a logic to Foot's opposition to German rearmament in the 1950s, and as the world came to understand the apocalyptic power of nuclear weapons, so Foot and *Tribune* were to become indelibly linked with the Campaign for Nuclear Disarmament and the Aldermaston Marches. When in 1957 his great hero Nye Bevan, whose hallowed Ebbw Vale seat Foot came to represent, told the Labour party conference that a commitment to unilateral nuclear disarmament would be a mistake that would, in effect, 'send a British foreign secretary naked into the conference chamber', their friendship survived the difference, even if the Tribunites in parliament were horribly riven.

There were other editors of *Tribune*, but *Tribune* and Michael Foot are synonymous. So many of the great campaigns – dismissed for being 'extreme' or 'minority causes' at the time but which went on to become the principled consensus – began there and with him: the campaign to boycott South African apartheid goods; the demand for a referendum on joining the then Common Market; and more recently, Foot and Craigie's great passion to save Bosnia and Kosovo both from Serbian ethnic cleansers and Western indifference. Foot was opposed to the Iraq war from the outset, and spoke passionately against it at the two-million-strong demonstration in Hyde Park.

An entire generation of anti-colonial activists – from Kenneth Kaunda and Walter Sisulu to Jomo Kenyatta and Cheddi Jagan, and before them, the Indian independence campaigners – were given space in *Tribune* at a time when the British government would rather have found space for them (and did) in prison. One of my proudest moments was when Nelson Mandela publicly thanked *Tribune* readers for their support during the apartheid era, and for their generosity in helping to build the school in Hout Bay, Cape Town, which he was there to open.

Foot, the man of peace, passed away peacefully. He will be mourned by friends and a few old foes alike, but mostly by his beloved family, his carers and especially Jenny Stringer, his friend and companion for many years. I shall remember him for his generosity and support and impish sense of humour.

Foot's support came in many ways, the most memorable being his 'takings' from that legal spat with Rupert Murdoch, which he gave to *Tribune*. Even though he has now finally left us, Michael will be delighted that *Tribune*, now in rude health, has survived both him and the banalities of New Labour. That said, he remained a firm supporter of his Labour party and of Gordon Brown, who frequently phoned him. Ever loyal to his occasionally idiosyncratic causes, Foot also remained a firm supporter of Plymouth Argyle.

There is, however, one contemporary and very sad truth which I know Foot understood and despaired about in equal measure: the dumbing-down and vacuity of modern British politics. Michael Foot, orator and parliamentarian beyond compare. Michael Foot, bibliophile, journalist and indefatigable demonstrator. Michael Foot, radical and socialist. That Michael Foot – even more so, the younger Michael Foot – would never be allowed to stand for parliament as a Labour candidate today, let alone lead the party.

Most of us are mere bystanders as the great events of state, of peace and war, pass us by. Throughout much of the last century Michael was an active participant, helping to shape those events, or better still challenging them.

I still keep the picture of Michael handing over a cheque which he had just received courtesy of Rupert Murdoch, after the *Sunday Times* had ludicrously libelled him as 'Agent Boot', friend of the Soviets.

This was not long after Michael had had a fall getting off the bus, blaming his black eye on 'Lurking Chetniks at King's Cross'.

We had another near mishap when Michael came to Buckingham to support me as Labour candidate in the general election in 2002. The back door of my old Jag swung open on a roundabout outside the town, and he almost fell out – but ever the old trouper he rallied, gave a vintage performance at the church hall, and was delighted when an elderly lady came up and planted a kiss on him, saying: 'We all fell in love with Michael back when he used to march with us and CND to Aldermaston.'

Michael Foot, when once asked what he would remember the most, said 'the demonstrations!' He was determined to speak at the Hyde Park demonstration against the Iraq war, despite his advanced years and failing mobility. I remember driving him all the way from Hampstead to Durham in the north-east for the annual Miners' Gala, with *Independent* journalist Sean O'Grady. Michael talked all of the way up, only pausing when we negotiated our way into Leicester from the M1, because Sean knew of a 'bloody good curry house' there. When we got to the County Hotel in Durham, we bumped into Tony Benn as we got out of the lift. Tony took one look at the slightly dishevelled Footie and said, 'Well, Michael, you should at least have put a tie on!' This slightly bristling interlude was of course rooted in a long and deep history of varying states of animosity between the two great men.

Not that all of the ex-miners and their families on the old Durham racecourse the next day seemed to mind. I had to follow the last of the colliery bands in the car with Michael in the passenger's seat. Progress was slow as successive hands reached through the window to clasp Michael. They loved him! It was like driving Mick Jagger through Hyde Park just before a gig. He was still looking forward to a return to the Durham Miners' Gala. He had what most contemporary politicians lack: an empathy that encouraged affection and reciprocation, a hinterland that was informed by his love of Swift, Byron, Hazlitt and Thomas Paine. Michael really was a Tribune of the People.

To the end he kept his impish wit, and shared the wisdom and knowledge drawn from a remarkable life spent with remarkable people.

How I miss him.

The strange death of radical journalism

AND SO TO another inconvenient truth that should trouble anyone interested in the clash of ideas, real passion in journalism, polemic and a radicalism worthy of its name. Iconic, radical journalism is on life-support in Britain. Michael Foot would have understood that, and his late, dear departed nephew Paul Foot already knew it before he passed on so prematurely.

To that decline can be added bold, risk-taking, analytical journalism and the depth that should come with it. Just where are those writers who have a broader world view, and who want to change it? Without what Karl Marx described as a dialectic, there is less trenchant, meaningful argument. Where is the bold, crusading *Daily Mirror*? When will the *Guardian* begin to emerge from its seemingly endless internal debate, and take up the cudgels? Who rails against conventional wisdom? And where are the journalists in that fine campaigning, irascible tradition of William Connor, Claud Cockburn and of course, Paul Foot?

The answer may be that they are out there somewhere in the

blogosphere, or maybe the best of them have given up altogether and gone to work in corporate PR. And while there are some that continue to hit the mark, all too often they are relegated and confined, since the bold newspaper editors of yesteryear have largely been replaced by over-cautious figures that live in fear of the bean-counters. Only the cartoonists are given free rein. Newspaper editors may wonder why their circulations keep falling. They may be tempted to blame the internet and belatedly erect paywalls that readers won't pay for. But their decline may be symptomatic of a deeper malaise. Just look at the wider retreat over the past twenty odd years. Serious in-depth coverage of Parliament has largely evaporated, although the *Daily Telegraph* recently gave it a timely boost over the expenses scandal.

There are few in-depth interviews of prominent political or public figures, and so much of the coverage is leavened parochialism of the 'who's up, who's down' variety, which also feeds directly into an increasingly comment driven BBC coverage. This is largely focussed on process and personality, and explains the obsession with imminent crisis and leadership challenge. In this race to the bottom, the political class like to dumb down to tabloid level, desperately trying, ties off, in mock Estuarial, to prove that it can mix it with 'the street'.

There are less resources for the investigative journalism that once characterised the *Sunday Times* 'Insight' pages, and of course there are fewer and fewer foreign correspondents, whose own depth of knowledge and understanding of different parts of the world once made some of them serious national figures. Foreign correspondents are of course expensive – or are they? The truth may lie some way in between, for massive amounts are squandered on anchors who need to be briefed as to where Somalia might be, or on the editor's favourite courtiers. The dwindling band of foreign correspondents, of whom I was once one, usually have to make do with far less, and work in far harder conditions that their domestic counterparts.

The twenty-four hour news culture hardly helps, but neither does the cost-cutting culture that puts poorly paid staff with remarkably little historical or folk memory in charge of the shape and direction of some of our newspapers. One veteran of the old *Daily Herald* and *Daily Mirror*, who operated at a time when typically there would be sixty staff on a news floor night shift instead of today's three, told me: 'We don't have many editors of real courage and stature, independent minded fighting spirits.' Although interestingly, he believes that the *Daily Mail's* Paul Dacre is a 'courageous editor' who runs against this trend, and he is right. Dacre knows what his readers want, but is also more than happy to mould them into believing something that may not necessarily have occurred to them. Like it or loathe it, the *Mail* knows its readership. It long ago left the *Express* in its wake, and the other red tops are all struggling. At Dacre Towers, the lights are only off one day a week. It reads well, is populist and relevant. But it is also very small 'c' conservative. The left used to have an antidote in the *Daily Mirror*, but the accountants haven't been good to it, nor was the reign of Piers Morgan, who was possibly the most shallow and ridiculous editor the Mirror has ever had.

I recently bumped into former Chancellor Alistair Darling minding his own business drinking a cup of tea in Parliament's Portcullis House. He had recently succeeded where most other Brits have failed, in getting published in the *New York Times* (which famously refused to take copy from Tony Blair when he was Prime Minister 'on grounds of quality'). Darling agreed with me that the British press now largely lacks the breadth and depth of analysis that can be found in some parts of the North American media. Which is not to take away from journalists such as Larry Elliott, Polly Toynbee, Jonathan Freedland, or heavyweight TV hitters such as Michael Crick or Paul Mason, but that for some of the most incisive, in-depth and occasionally humorous writing, some editors turn to American writers such as Frank Rich, Paul Krugman and E.J. Dionne to fill the domestic void. Although the *Guardian* has on occasion tried to ape the *New York Times*, we have little of that fine New York tradition here – still less the informative longer essays, reviews and investigations that are such a feature of many of the *New Yorker*, *Atlantic* or *Vanity Fair*.

And then of course there has been the cloying, unbelievably dreary reduction of so much political journalism and commentary to the lowest denomination party politics and politicians who have littered Westminster these past two decades, droning on about the 'Third Way' and writing 'memos' to one another, hoping to be spotted and patted. And here, in the so called 'centre ground' of consensual journalism and politics, we have seen some of the worst offences. There has a grown a deep prejudice towards virtually any writer who goes against conventional wisdom, whether it be John Pilger on the left or Simon Heffer on the right. They are dismissed as extreme, or bonkers, or both – a convenient way of closing down argument without having to display any. Indeed, some months after writing this chapter and coming to edit it, Simon Heffer, an honest and forthright critic of David Cameron and the Coalition, had been bumped by the *Daily Telegraph*.

This drive for consensus has been aided and abetted by journalists who provided 'intellectual' justification for the New Labour project, and who are now doing the same as the British political class settles around the new Cameron dispensation. Andrew Marr's history of modern Britain TV series was a classic example of this, as are many of the columns of David Aaronovitch,

Andrew Rawnsley, Martin Kettle and John Rentoul – all of whom the late Michael Foot would have enjoyed mocking and exposing in his heyday.

Marr is a particular case in point. The BBC's 'wunderkind' famously came unstuck when Ian Hislop and *Private Eye* could remain silent no longer about one of the much talked-of 'gagging orders' that had prevented any reporting of an affair between Marr and a journalist on *The Times* for eight years – a gag that the Marr family had taken out. The idea of journalists having affairs with one another will hardly come as a shock, but when news of the 'gagging order' came on top of Marr's interrogation of Gordon Brown, as to whether the Prime Minister was taking mood-influencing drugs, Marr reached a new low in double standards. In fact a trawl through Marr's sofa-driven Sunday morning interrogations reveals a bullying drive to embarrass public figures over all sorts of alleged peccadilloes. So the idea that Marr should hide behind a 'gagging order' is beyond parody. But then, as many of us knew, Marr had not only paid through the nose for the gagging order, he was still helping out the mother of a child that was not his but that of a former Labour minister.

But Marr's stock in trade as the 'Uriah Heep' of Westminster was of applying a fairly lightweight veneer of intellectual respectability over Tony Blair, and his Third Way in particular. The cult of Marr was largely of the BBC and Marr's own creation, and is essentially evidence of the intellectual decline of a great journalistic institution. And Marr, had he not been so insufferable, and had he not always ignored those who weren't important enough for him to talk to, might just have found his own landing a little softer.

(Cartoonist Martin Rowson recalls that Marr was a particularly active supporter of the Trotskyite Socialist Organiser sect at Cambridge University: 'We liked to call this bunch the 'Soggy

Oggies', as they regarded themselves as a cut above the less *avant-garde* and more working-class Militant Tendency. Back then in the early 1980s, Marr sported a small goatee beard, of the sort once favoured by Trotsky himself. He wore a reefer jacket similar to the one worn by men in the Parks Departments or those who worked for the National Coal Board. This was all set off by a blue, Lenin-style cap, and Marr would peddle copies of his organ around the campus. On one occasion he clearly got up the nose of some of his fellow students, because they chucked him into a pond.' I loved this tale because it neatly summed up the political trajectory of so many journalists and politicians who either supported or were part of New Labour. The prerequisite for being in any far Left sect, as Marr would know, is to 'follow the line'. Of course by the time Marr had joined *The Economist* his youthful enthusiasm would have faded, but that didn't stop me from asking Rowson to depict student Marr during his revolutionary heyday for a *Tribune* cartoon. As with the *Eye*'s less than sparing use of a picture depicting Andrew Neil and a party-going babe, I published 'Red Andy' at every opportunity. In the end he bought the offending item, claiming to have put it up in his lavatory – but I wonder if he didn't flush the thing down it.)

Stymied in Stoke

COULD IT REALLY have been five years since I was in this city? And had anything actually changed in that time to a place that had never really recovered from the great wave of industrial closures and contractions of the 1980s? The answers was: not really that much. Except that most people I spoke to in Stoke-on-Trent had become even more disillusioned with the political class, so much so that they had begun to elect councillors from the British National Party, and the Labour Party was but a rump in what the psephologists and commentators like to call a 'Labour heartland'. You have to have a heart to have a land in which it beats, and Labour's was now reduced to a dull, spluttering, murmur. The 2010 General Election was weeks away and the Westminster media wanted to tell us that it could be a 'game-changing' election – but here in Stoke whatever happened would probably mean more of the same, or worse. I couldn't see any sign of political activity whatsoever – except on a ripped hoarding outside a ramshackle theatre squatting in between boarded up shops in Hanley. It advertised a recent film and discussion on the miners' strike that had taken place a quarter of a century ago, announcing the participation of 'Ken Loach, George Galloway and Edwina Currie'. I wondered idly how they would all have got on as they sipped tea from chipped mugs, standing on sticky, worn carpets. 'It was packed', said former Labour councillor and activist Mick Williams, whom I met for a mug of tea in Tescos and who was shortly to rip up his membership card in a final act of protest at the control freaks. Paradoxically, he had recently been awarded a Labour Party Merit Award for Long Service from Gordon Brown.

I remembered debating with Edwina Currie and Simon Heffer at Trinity College, Dublin. 'Do you know what I found most irritating about Currie?', I asked Mick: 'The way she always referred to her constituents as "my miners" or "my car workers". As if anyone would want to belong to her!'

'John Major did!', said Mick spryly.

'Which reminds me', said I, 'I knew about the John Major and Edwina Currie Ugandan discussions before the story broke, because Dennis Skinner told me. Dennis had been told all of the gory details by a cleaning lady who looked after Major's flat in Dolphin Square'.

To be honest I didn't really want to be here, parked outside the 'Seddon Stadium', Stoke City's home football ground – even though this could have been interpreted as a lucky porten. Nothing to do with the city. I liked the no-nonsense, 'find us like we are' attitude of Stokies. The place had history and it had pride. No, in my heart this felt like a re-run, another humiliation in the making. You have to really know the Labour Party, or what has become of it, to understand the low cunning and base motivations of those who wield power, imaginary or not, in a party from which power was now very visibly ebbing away. The New Labour years had come to be defined, as Clare Short so aptly put it to me, by a 'very special degree of venom and nastiness', an environment where inevitably many of those who had prospered were deeply unpleasant, or had had to become deeply unpleasant to survive. I had come to meet Barry Stockley, the careworn, put-upon chairman of the Stoke Central Labour Party, whose depiction of an equally worn rump of a local Labour Party, washed out and wrung out and in a constant losing battle of attrition with New Labour control freaks, seemed sadly familiar. 'This is a left-of-centre party, what's left of it,' said Barry, an amiable Stoke patriot whose reward for decades of hard work was yet more punishment from a cabal out to get him: 'You would be just the right sort to be our candidate here.'

Which is more or less what Labour's Chief Whip Nick Brown had said to me a week or so before, when I went to see him in his eyrie in the House of Commons. 'We need someone with some street credibility there in Stoke,' said Nick, 'the party is in a right mess' – at which point he picked up a sheaf of papers from the bin and said, 'Take a look at these, but you can't take them with you.' The bunch of papers contained shrill warnings for 'urgent action' from paid party officials against the handful of troublesome pensioners remaining in the Stoke Labour Party who had so successfully derailed the Blairite plan to have an elected Mayor – an idea Stokies sensibly hadn't taken too either, and kicked out in a referendum, the first of its type. 'And of course,' said Nick, 'the BNP are on the rise there, and we need someone to take them on. You'll have to get your sleeves rolled up.' Which all reminded me of a conversation I had had with Nick well over a decade ago in a pub overlooking the sweep of the Tyne in his constituency. I had been helping him in a cause I knew meant more to him that many other MPs in the North East – desperately trying to get the Major government to step in and save the Swan Hunter shipyard from closure. We knew back then that if Labour finally managed to get back, it would have to move quickly in places like Newcastle where the good, skilled, comparatively well paid jobs were still in the process of going – and where the far Right would attempt to fill the breach. Just as they were doing in Stoke now.

'But what will stop them from blocking me yet again?', I pressed Nick. 'I'll ask to see your CV, so that will stop them from shredding it. Anyhow, Blair is gone now, and who cares about him any more? Gordon likes you, and this idea that people like you and [John] Cryer pose a threat is ridiculous. We are going to have more problems from some of those who are about to get in who have no politics at all.' Nick then opened the door into the whips' office, which I suppose was a way of showing the real hard men of Labour politics that a blessing of sorts had been conferred. John Spellar grinned and pushed a copy of the *Daily Mirror* to one side. I wondered if Spellar had any inkling that soon after canvassing for Peter Tatchell in Bermondsey all those years ago, I had gone and campaigned for him in his by-election in Birmingham Northfields in 1982? The Labour whips' office is a bit like a sergeants' mess, except that instead of pictures of the Queen, there are framed portraits of people like Margaret Beckett.

The meeting with Nick hadn't happened by chance. A week earlier, Labour's good and great, of which Nick was one, had been gathered at Golders Green Crematorium for the funeral of Michael Foot. The family had asked me to speak, and so I had ransacked Michael's seminal *Guilty Men* for some choice quotes, hoping to prick a few consciences as I knew Alastair Campbell and others were going to show up. I had also heard that Cherie Blair was going to make a cameo appearance. She called to say that since Mary Wilson (widow of Harold) was coming and might need some assistance, could she come with her? So there we all were, sitting in a line: me, Bruce Kent, John Foot, Matt Foot and Neil Kinnock staring disconsolately at Michael's simple coffin, across which were arranged a green and white Plymouth Argyle scarf – the one Michael always wore to the *Tribune* office – and a bunch of red roses. I still couldn't believe that the ageless Footie, with his warmth, wit, passion and zest of life had finally departed. With him gone, so was my old friend and protector. Matt said of his great-uncle: 'The thing with Michael was his eternal optimism, his zest and enthusiasm for everything – even his boiled egg in the morning! It was always "the best boiled egg in the world, EVER!" And when one day recently there was no boiled egg for breakfast, I heard Michael exclaim, "I'm still protesting!"'

I could picture him, spoon waving, sort of missing the egg, and then colliding with it and with a giant scoop and a swoop, its top being lifted off triumphantly. 'Ahhh!! Ayeee!!', would have been the triumphant Foot cry.

And then in came Gordon Brown. I hadn't seen Gordon close up for three or four years, and since I was speaking after him, he plumped down in the pew next to me. This was after he had shaken everyone's hand with the peremptory Gordon greeting of 'How yer doin?' He was parchment pale, with huge bags under his eyes, but he had come armed with a speech he had clearly spend much time writing himself, all in that big loopy print that he needs to be able to read – and without glasses – from his one good eye. Michael had liked Gordon very much, and the last time I had seen him in his Hampstead sitting room he had waved Gordon and Sarah's Christmas card around rather proudly: in fact Michael had been pictured by the *Hampstead and Highgate Express* as it was it delivered. For his part, Gordon delighted in the old bibliophile's company on the occasions that he got to see him, which were not very often.

Gordon turned to me. 'What are yer doin?' I mumbled something about writing for various papers and doing a bit of broadcasting. 'You need to be in Parliament!', he barked. But somehow – perhaps it was the passage of time, or was it the fact that Gordon was a past master at all of this? – I dimly recall smiling wanly, and muttered something about 'Stoke-on-Trent', and Gordon sort of muttering something back. A promise from Gordon, you see, has to be taken with a pinch of salt. His speech, as it turned out, roused the old Labour faithful. It stopped all of the moaners in their tracks and momentarily reminded them of why they had joined this 'GMO' – 'Great Movement of Ours' – in the first place. Gordon was the paramount chief, versed in Shelley and Byron and all of the socialist greats. He even managed to upstage Neil Kinnock, who has that rare gift of Welsh oratory, when he remembers not to overdo it. Now I have watched Gordon make a speech to the Bevan Society in Pontypridd and go immediately afterwards and deliver a completely different speech to the CBI. Even so, on this day, even Gordon would have found it near impossible to go from the celebration that was the funeral of the great man Footie to, shall we say, a memorial for Margaret Thatcher – who, lest we forget, he had over to Downing Street well before he had Michael. A crime it has to be said he was repeating, as Blair had the 'Great She Elephant' over, as Denis Healey once called her, before he invited James Callaghan, who was a former Labour Prime Minister.

But I immediately relayed what Gordon had said to me to Nick Brown and the retiring MP for Stoke, Mark Fisher, in the Crematorium garden. This followed a cursory discussion with Alastair Campbell, at his instigation, about my tie, which, given the occasion, was black. Alastair said that Michael didn't go in much for ties, still less for black ones – on which point he may be right. And since this was probably the most cordial interaction I have ever had with Alastair, we had best leave it there.

Nick and Mark both urged me to throw my hat in the ring. 'They'll love you there,' said Mark: 'They are a really good bunch of people. I'm just so sorry to have to be leaving them all when they need all of the support they can get.' Mark had recently had a major operation, and really couldn't stand again, bravely as he had withstood the pressure at the last election from the control freaks, when he was promised a peerage if he would make way for a 'parachuted-in' candidate.

What I didn't know, of course, was that one mighty big silk parachute was in the process of being attached to none other than television historian Tristram Hunt, whom most people were nice about, albeit prefacing their remarks about 'how a bloke with a name like Tristram will go down in Stoke' and generally decrying his lack of party experience.

Suffice to say, in any straight contest I was sure that I would have a decent chance of getting adopted, but once again, I had made the fatal mistake of underestimating the determination of Peter Mandelson, who was a pal of Hunt's. Keith Vaz, chairman of what without any hint of irony was called the 'Special Selections Panel' and who had been a great supporter of mine over Stoke, told me, after I had not even been asked for an interview: 'Mark, it was a Mandelson ask.' Translated, this meant that Mandelson had asked Gordon for Stoke to be 'given' to Tristram. Gordon had immediately agreed this request from the man who had once been his most poisonous enemy – and the 'Special Selections Panel' duly obliged by fixing the selection process for Tristram, at which point a number of the remaining activists walked out for good. Stoke-on-Trent had become the quintessential New Labour 'rotten borough', where Stokies were supposed to vote for anything in a red rosette. I wrote a letter to Mandelson, and then junked it. What was the point? The man was only in it for himself, and always had been. The best hope of finally getting shot of him would be when we lost the election.

Keith later told me that the other two members of the panel – names I hadn't even heard of – had turned me down on the hilarious pretext that 'since he is working in New York, he won't be seen as local.' That is of course what they had been ordered to say.

I subsequently wrote a personal letter to Gordon Brown requesting, given his support for me in our conversation in the crematorium, that he arrange for me at least to be interviewed, but never received a reply.

My Stoke experience was repeated elsewhere in the country by New Labour and Cameron's Conservatives alike, although Cameron was far less successful. Place-men and -women, candidates who can be relied upon to toe the line, who have no dangerous thoughts, still less a history – these are the people of Britain's technocratic political classes. Is it any wonder that Parliament has become stuffed with clones and Stepford wives? Is it any wonder that the political class has become so despised?

I haven't seen Gordon Brown since the General Election, although I did once spot Sarah crossing the road near Dean's Yard in Westminster, and I had the impression that she was pretending not to see me. I guess I have known Gordon since the early 1990s, and worked with him on and off while broadly describing myself as a 'critical friend' of his. The trouble is that he was never that good at looking after his friends. Nevertheless history will treat him more kindly than Tony Blair, since when it came to halting a global slide into depression, Gordon was in the right place at the right time.

A President calls ...

TO BE A journalist is to have a grandstand view of life, and to have been involved in politics as well may damn you in 'Little Britain', but it can lead to some wonderful opportunities to attempt to practise a bit of both. And this is what happened when the President of the Maldives called in the late Summer of 2010. Mohammed Nasheed, or 'Anni' as he is known to friends, is the country's first elected President, having been held in prison and on one notorious occasion tortured by the previous regime of President Gayoom – a Ba'athist by trade. In a PR master stroke, he held his first Cabinet meeting underwater to demonstrate the likely effects of global warming on these low lying atolls.

I first met Anni with my old school friend Dave Hardingham in London when they came to the *Tribune* office in Hampstead. Coincidentally, Anni had also been at Dauntseys School, although after me, and the Hardingham family had been key supporters during the long, dark years of dictatorship. While British politicians continued to jet off to the Maldives, the Hardinghams helped Anni and his friends in their home city of Salisbury, which for a time was the unofficial HQ of the Maldives opposition.

We gave space to Anni in *Tribune* and I used to make a point of reminding John Prescott and Hilary Armstrong, as they prepared to jet off to the Ba'athist Maldives, that while doing so they were apparently content to bomb Ba'athist Baghdad, probably earning their undying hatred in the process.

So when, as President of these scattered isles in the Indian Ocean, Anni decided to go after some of the millions stashed away in foreign banks by the old regime, some of Gayoom's old henchmen, in combination with a corrupted judiciary still stuffed with supporters of the former regime, did their utmost to destabilise the new government, and after offering to write an article on their activities I was summoned to visit the President.

Male', the capital, has the distinction of being one of the most crowded places on the planet – all two square miles of it crammed full of buildings. Anni could have decanted to one of Gayoom's former sumptuous homes on one of the outlying islands, but he chose to base himself in the 'bungalow', a fairly unprepossessing building which has as its centre piece an older building that was once used by the Sultan. This is where I would later interview Anni for Al Jazeera TV.

Anni jumped up and urged me over to a long, low table with chairs in the courtyard – just the sort of place that I could imagine Tony Blair loving, a sort of sofa government of the tropics.

'The EU have offered to send some auditors to help track down the missing millions,' he said, showing me his Blackberry. 'Should I accept?' This was the sort of question to which the person asking has long ago decided the answer already, but of course it had the desired effect on me. Anni is quite diminutive and his intellect cuts like a knife through hot butter. He had decided to put one leading opposition member and racketeer under house arrest for a few days, earning a lightning visit from a US Special Envoy who urged that the President 'respect the Constitution', and a similar encomium from the UK Foreign Office, which I had been asked to convey to Anni, since former Foreign Office minister Denis MacShane had told them I was going to the Maldives.

'I now know what it is like to use authoritarian powers,' said Anni. 'It would be very easy to become a dictator. But you need to know that this is absolutely not what I want to do. I want to build our young democracy here.'

I wondered if he should go for early election to try and flush out the old kleptocrats, as well as maybe holding a referendum on constitutional reform – 'But you have to know you will win,' I said rather lamely. Of course, Anni had already thought about that.

Since it was Independence Day – forty-five years since the Maldives had ceased to be a British protectorate – it was also grand opening day in Male': the grand opening of the brand new National Museum for starters. 'That looks like a Chinese bank!', I said to my guide Shaheda, and had the reply: 'That's because it has been built by the Chinese as a gift.' As was the spanking new civil service offices near the harbour, again built on time with Chinese labour by a Chinese company. Fortunately for the Maldives, just as the global recession kicked in the Chinese appeared to have discovered the Maldives on the web. The Chinese ambassador told me that over 60,000 holiday makers had come there in the last year alone. My next door neighbours at the resort where I was staying were a friendly family from Beijing. 'I just hope they don't hear that we have lots of sharks here. The Chinese like shark fin soup,' murmured a Maldivian foreign office official as the ambassador cut the red ribbon on the big shiny museum.

The Battle for Buckingham: Part 2 – The 2010 General Election

HAVING BEEN PREVENTED yet again from standing as a Labour candidate, I got a call from a friend of John Stevens, former Conservative MEP turned Liberal Democrat, whom I recalled seeing on television in the past. Stevens was a very strong pro-European, and although I wasn't an EU enthusiast, he always made a good case. In any event, I was told, he was going to challenge John Bercow as an independent. Would I go like to have lunch with him? Since there wasn't a Labour Party candidate, I was free to do what I wanted.

I liked Stevens, while I had also become more and more irritated with John Bercow over his house-flipping, as revealed in the parliamentary expenses scandal of 2009. But it was a different matter to go out and nominate Stevens and canvass for him. Despite my irritation at Bercow, I recalled that both he and his wife Sally had come to lunch at our house, and that my late uncle Roger Henderson, had been quite a supporter of his (so much so that there is still a picture of a much younger Bercow stuck on the wall of my uncle's old study). Also in mitigation, John Bercow had been around to visit my aunt at my instigation over some issue or other, after which we had all gone for a walk. I realised then that the future Mr Speaker had never quite adapted to the countryside, because on spotting a group of young pheasants he asked, 'What are they?'

Before I committed to help Stevens, I thought I would test the water, partly by seeing what friends and neighbours thought. I wrote a piece for the *Evening Standard* which somehow got lost in all the election coverage and was never published, but it gives a flavour of the early stage of what was a fairly dramatic and colourful election:

Deep in the Buckinghamshire countryside something is stirring. Even before the General Election campaign begins, leaflets are beginning to drop through letterboxes and the letters pages of local newspapers are unusually lively. This is natural small 'c' conservative territory. It always has been, bar a brief sojourn for the 'bouncing Czech', Robert Maxwell, and a Labour MP when the Buckingham constituency included Bletchley, once also home to the wartime Enigma codebreakers. So Conservative territory it may be, but the local MP John Bercow is now Mr Speaker, so a Tory representative no longer, and all of a sudden he faces an insurgency.

In what is promising to be one of the most closely fought and bitter General Elections in living memory, the upcoming 'Battle for Buckingham' is set to provide colour and entertainment in equal measure. Two prominent figures are squaring up to Mr Speaker Bercow, and seemingly underpinning their challenge are serious constitutional issues, and bubbling away underneath all of that is the national sense of outrage at the Westminster gravy train.

Speaker Bercow for his part will doubtlessly affect to swat away these impudent arrivistes, in the knowledge that many think he has served the area well.

Step forward then, Nigel Farage, the pinstriped telegenic of UKIP fame, who has recently set up camp in some well appointed offices in Buckingham town centre, and who recently took charge of an ill fated UKIP attempt to wrest control of a local council seat from the Tories. Step forward also former MEP turned independent candidate John Stevens, whose attack on John Bercow's expense claims has been plastered across local newspaper front pages in recent days. Farage says of the expenses row: 'We are witnessing the last remaining reels of a particularly grisly horror movie.' He has pronounced Speaker Bercow as 'Mr Very Pleased With Himself', and has promised voters that he will have 'a drink in every pub in the constituency.' This would amount to some twenty pints a day on conservative estimates. This promise has galvanised John Bercow into responding: 'I accept that sadly some now see politics as a bit of a lark – perhaps politicians have only themselves to blame. But Buckingham deserves better than being treated as a glorified pub crawl or media event.'

The old convention says that Mr Speaker stands unchallenged by the main political parties, and while Labour and the Liberal Democrats are sticking to this, one of the main charges of both Farage and Stevens is that Buckingham, like an old rotten borough, would otherwise be deprived of having both a choice of candidates and an active MP in the House of Commons. John Stevens has taken this a stage further saying, 'Mr Bercow has made no attempt to justify his abuse of the expenses system, including his avoidance of Capital Gains Tax, through house "flipping", which has continued even after his election as Speaker on a supposed platform of reform. It is for this reason that he is a symbol of this discredited Parliament, and must be defeated.' Stevens has enlisted the support of Flipper the Dolphin, the children's television character, and promises that 'Flipper', a man dressed in a dolphin's costume, will be making numerous public appearances to ram his message home.

This part of the world would normally be described as leafy – if it were summertime. It is certainly bucolic.

This is also the territory of the Bicester and Whaddon Hunt, which once registered little local interest, but since the hunt ban seems to have become very popular with cussed locals who don't like being bossed about. Ironically, when Tony Blair and his wife Cherie came house-hunting in the area, they alighted first on the forbidding Winslow Hall in the small town of the same name, until, as local folklore goes, someone told them that the Boxing Day meet takes place outside the place.

Tony and Cherie settled on Sir John Gielgud's old pile a few miles away as the crow flies, and would-be candidates will doubtlessly be beating a path to their doors as the election approaches. As they will no doubt to Waddesdon Manor, home to the Rothschilds, and apparently in whose grounds Business Secretary Lord Mandelson went on a shoot not so long ago. Who or what he shot remains a matter of local conjecture. Waddesdon Manor is famous for many things, not least an ill-fated Foreign Office inspired stopover for a French President who was reportedly furious when he discovered how much French art and antiques were in Buckinghamshire rather than Paris, and also as backdrop for the film Carry On Don't Lose Your Head.

If anyone ever makes a film of 'The Battle for Buckingham', perhaps they will call it Carry on Canvassing, for in addition to the Blairs there are the Duncan Smiths, who preside over the Cottesloe Estate around Swanbourne. As befits a country estate, all of the house doors in Swanbourne are painted olive green, so plenty of scope here for a few mistakes involving candidates and leaflets. Not for nothing was Iain Duncan Smith known as the 'quiet man'. Sometimes he may be spotted nipping incognito into an Indian takeaway in nearby Winslow, to order his regular chicken tikka biryani. Once when the Conservatives did well in local elections, he ordered a whole stack of chicken tikka biriyanis. Given IDS' fame and notoriety, I tried for some time to persuade the local restaurant owner to put up a picture of him, but was told that customers might get him mixed up with the late Panchen Lama of Tibet. Either way, IDS and his family have certainly added to the gaiety of life, for as pubs are boarded up the length and breadth of the land, the Cottesloe Estate boasts a new pub, the Betsy Wynne, where the candidates will be able to quaff a few ales at the end of a long day on the stump. Perhaps they will spot IDS.

But Buckingham is not all toffs and big houses. To the south of the constituency is Cheddington, a railway stop where the Royal Mail train was famously stopped by Ronnie Biggs and the 'Great Train Robbers' forty-odd years ago. And there are plenty of voters not so steeped in the Conservative Party who have made the trek out of London over the past decades, bringing their voting habits with them. New estates ribbon Buckingham, Winslow and Haddenham, and coming into the constituency for the first time is Princes Risborough, which may prove fertile ground for the would be Bercow challengers.

If the former Chinese premier Chou En Lai when famously asked about the effects of the French Revolution could respond to the question, 'It is too early to tell,' only a fool could pretend to predict what might happen in Buckingham in a month or so. At face value, John Bercow has a seemingly impregnable majority with over 57 per cent of the vote at the last election and it will be difficult to dislodge him. But as Speaker he cannot rely on the local

Conservative Party machine, much of which will be despatched by Tory Central Office – no friends of Mr Speaker there – to try and drive out Milton Keynes' surviving Labour MP. Bercow will be able to rely on a network of Conservative district and county councillors, as well as those who think he is an assiduous MP, or those that think he is being sniped at unfairly. Bercow says: 'Each of the three main parties supports my re-election campaign, and David Cameron has urged all Conservative voters, as well as voters of other parties, to vote for me.'

So much in the end may boil down to whether voters vote, and if they do, what will motivate them. John Bercow is accused of 'flipping' his property, avoiding capital gains tax and claiming the maximum amount of MPs' allowances. Even in relatively well-heeled Buckingham, this rubs. Scarcely a week has gone by without fresh, lurid national headlines, involving Mr Speaker's £45,000 spend on Mr Speaker's grace-and-favour flat, the employment of a press officer at a cost to the taxpayer of £107,000, and the hire of an accountant to fill in his returns – at our expense – of a £1,000.

All of this is taken from a leaflet that has recently dropped through the door, courtesy of John Stevens, who is also something of a Civil War buff. If I am reading it, so are many others in Buckingham, and some of them will recall that this part of the World once produced fine Cromwellian Lieutenants such as John Hampden. Their revolt was as much about the king as it was the rotten Parliaments, and when it comes to ripe rottenness, there is not much to compare to our Parliament today. If former Speaker Michael Martin came to be seen as symbolic of that Parliament, John Bercow, to his critics at least, has played his part in the Commons' expense claims culture.

The new 'Battle for Buckingham' is about to be joined!

For the record, John Bercow won the seat fairly convincingly, while John Stevens surprised many by pushing Nigel Farage into third place.

The parents of Iain Duncan Smith's wife might well have voted for John Stevens rather than John Bercow, but then plenty of the old shire Tories did just that. As for IDS, ever the quiet man, who knows? I meant to ask him the last time I saw him standing in the queue at a Winslow petrol station, but then thought better of it.

Students doth protest!

SEEING ASSORTED YOBS smash up Conservative Central Office – or rather what they thought was Conservative Central Office – in 2010, looking at them daubing a venerable Gilbert Scott red telephone box and setting fire to a bus shelter, my first thought was, 'Send in the riot squad and teach 'em all a lesson!' My second thought was, 'Oh hell, I've become a middle-aged fart, and forgotten that I was once a student radical!' And then I started thinking of all of some of those other radical students – a bit before my time – that once showed us the way: Jack Straw, Charles Clarke, Trevor Phillips, Andrew Marr, Sue Slipman, David Aaronovitch. The latter pair were CP-ers, as they were known (Communists to you and me).

The late 1960s and early 1970s were the radical heyday of militant student unionism. Students were forever occupying the Dean's Office, going on rent strikes and supporting good causes like CND and an end to the American war in Vietnam. One of the more memorable sit-ins was at the Hornsey College of Art, led in part by one Kim Howells, another leather-jacketed CP-er who like so many former Commies and Trots became trenchant Stalinists in reverse by becoming New Labour.

But never mind all of these boring middle-aged farts, who will all probably be suffering amnesia as to what they really got up to on the protests and picket lines. Red Lion Square, the Grosvenor Square riot, the sit-ins and marches of the Sixties and Seventies had seemingly passed into history – until Maggie won the election in 1979. Then as now, there was unrest on the streets and a Royal Wedding planned to take our minds away from the misery of the lengthening dole queues. And then Thatcher and her government decided to bring in student loans. Suddenly the stage was set for a student upsurge, and by good fortune I had been elected as President of the University of East Anglia Students' Union.

This was 1984. My year in preparation had begun with the arrival of some flying pickets from the Durham coalfield, who perfected their 'Zulu warrior' war dance in front of bewildered members of the Norwich constabulary. At the time, the small dock in Norwich was being used to unload coal from Poland. I followed them back to their native picket lines, hitching up to the freezing North-East, to Dawdon, Easington and the marvellously named Vane Tempest Colliery. This was a struggle in the raw, far away from the video cameras and mobile phones of today, where grown men didn't bleat and cry when they got nicked and kicked. But they got their revenge one day when a few of them dressed a snow-covered hydrant as a picket, lobbed some stones at the coppers, only to cheer as a police van drove into it.

Each week, we corralled student union vans to take food and provisions to striking miners over at Ollerton in the Nottinghamshire coalfield, and back came some of the miners came to the university. On one occasion, we hired a big red double-decker bus to take assorted miners, members of Norwich Trades Council and spotty students down to Wivenhoe port, where coal was also being imported. Years later, while writing a piece for *Country Life* on 'punt gunning in the Blackwater Estuary', the fellow I recounted the story to, my guide and companion as we paddled across the marshes in search of geese, loudly exploded: 'But I was the bloody harbour master at the time!'

I think I must have been on about a dozen demos that year in 1984, all largely peaceful: against the loans; for nuclear disarmament; for jobs and for the miners. Other highlights included the flour-bombing of Cecil Parkinson and trouble for the chairman of the student Labour Club – he was the son of an Anglican bishop – for describing Parkinson as a 'Potent Prick' in the student newspaper. Then of course there was the mass demonstration in London, where a large body of students sat down and blocked Westminster Bridge while the then President of the NUS, one Phil Woolas, stood on a bus shelter, megaphone in hand, urging his members to behave, which is largely what they did.

In the years since, generations of ex-student radicals went into politics and set about kicking the higher education ladder away. So much so that tuition fees are already the highest of any country in the European Union, and are set to go through the stratosphere. Of course, today's student protestors, bar the small mob of yobs bent on smashing everything up, are a much more civilised bunch. They don't seem to want to change the world or support each and every radical campaign under the sun, which is a bit of a disappointment. Instead of shouting, 'A Marxist analysis is what we want!', they more mutely cry, 'A market analysis is what we, er, want!' For genuine, unapologetic radicals like Tariq Ali, this must be pretty galling. But then, as any former Marxists like 'Red' Andy Marr and David Aaronovitch will know, the crushed, squeezed middle classes can be a whole lot more dangerous than the downtrodden workers.

Remember them?

Invisible Labour

IF POLITICS GOES in cycles, and it's only the big crises such as war or economic depression that gets the wheel revolving in a different direction, then the cobbled together Coalition that emerged from the wreckage of the Labour Government in May 2010 is possibly just the first judder of that wheel. The banking crisis was answered by the return of Keynesian economic pump-priming, and on a massive scale, particularly in the United States. In the UK, Gordon Brown finally realised that his mantra of 'No return to boom and bust' was just another load of baloney, courtesy of Alan Greenspan of the Federal Reserve and Ed Balls. And fortuitously the bank bail-out was accompanied by a continued pre-election spending on the public services, thus insulating voters from the horrors that would come from over-hasty deficit reduction, and massive spending cuts. 'Endogenous growth theory' went to the same place as the 'Third Way' – the shredding machine. Those who championed it, along with 'soft touch regulation', suddenly changed tack and pretended never to have done so.

To escape from the surreal madness of the 2010 General Election campaign in Buckingham, I went up to Sherwood in

Nottinghamshire to support Labour's young candidate Emily Oldknow, who was a Midlands party official and the partner of Jonathan Ashworth, a thoughtful young aide to Gordon Brown, who in 2011 won a by-election in Leicester. I knew the area well, and was sent off to the old mining town of Ollerton to do some canvassing. Within a few minutes I had bumped into some characters that I had last seen quarter of a century ago at the height of the miners' strike. It was largely the sons and daughters of ex-miners, particularly the minority striking miners of Nottinghamshire that put up the placards and bill posters for Emily. It was proving to be a tough fight in a constituency that D.H. Lawrence would still recognise in part: the wealthy rural farming areas and the old industrial towns that had grown up in the shadow of the forest. It was refreshing to see that Labour could field a smart young candidate and have a coterie of supporters of all ages out on the stump for her. In the end, on election night, there was a recount, as Emily Oldknow had lost by barely 200-odd votes. I was left thinking that really the Tories should have been on a roll here and in other places, but hadn't managed to pack the killer punch. Of course they had massively spent in many other areas, but even so, their lack of a mandate was some sort of credit to the way in which the Labour Party fought back in the last days of the campaign. It seemed that the public had largely tired of the endless squabbling of New Labour, but was fearful of what lay around the corner. People were still not persuaded that Cameron and Osborne could lift Britain out of the deep morass into which it had sunk.

But Gordon wasn't going to get any credit for sticking his finger in the dyke, albeit with shed loads of our money. So it was that voters gave Labour a terrible kicking, pushing the party back to a result that was marginally worse than 1983, and finally liberating poor old Michael Foot from the ignominy of always being referred to as the poorest performing Labour leader ever. That honour was now conferred on Gordon. But what voters didn't do was to give David Cameron, another product from the Blair production line, his overall majority. Instead they conveyed the role of kingmaker to yet another product from the Blair production line, Nick Clegg, who had bizarrely wooed voters with his hand clasping and winsome ability to look the camera in the eye during the first ever TV debates. Ask anyone what Clegg actually said immediately after those 'debates' ended, and they wouldn't have a clue.

I had been asked to write a profile about Nick Clegg for a New York magazine during the General Election, and had found myself looking blankly at my screen for an hour or so, before I went out to dig the vegetable patch. There just didn't seem to be anything there. I occasionally used to see him hunched in deep conversation with former MP and Tory commentator Matthew Parris in the Gay Hussar, and Matthew, who always seemed to be a reasonable judge of character, told me he thought highly of him. And of course Clegg seemed and sounded a 'nice sort of bloke'. Watching him perform on the television, and following the ridiculous gushing from assorted hacks and hackettes, it seemed genuinely difficult to know what Cleggy was going on about. What on earth was all the fuss?

During the election campaign, Simon Hoggart once again came up to Buckingham to write a sketch about independent candidate John Stevens' brave – but ultimately foolhardy – attempt to defenestrate our house-flipping, capital gains tax-avoiding Speaker John Bercow. In pursuit of votes, I thought we should take the media caravan up to Tony and Cherie's pile at Wotton, a beautiful Rothschild house once owned by a real actor in Sir John Gielgud, as opposed to the actor-manager Blair. As our cavalcade marched up the drive, followed in quick succession by my friend Richard Jones, the performance artist dressed as Flipper the Dolphin, and a white-suited Martin Bell, Hoggart expressed amazement that Cleggy was in some quarters being compared with Obama. 'I was at a school the other day, and there was definitely a kind of Obama buzz,' said Simon. 'The kids appeared genuinely excited that Clegg was coming – this kind of pop star celeb. He arrived to all of this cheering. And then he spoke: "Point one … drone … point two … drone … point three", and by this time the whole thing had subsided like a pricked bubble.' (Tony Blair wasn't in when we knocked.)

Perhaps that is what will happen to Cleggy, Cameron, Osborne and their coalition. I can't see Lib Dem activists on the ground, especially those who have spent decades fighting bitter battles with Tories in Southern England, going along with this cabal for too long. But then, maybe Cleggy isn't that bothered. He could seamlessly move to the Tories, as a kind of 'National Liberal' when the going gets even tougher.

Meanwhile Labour, fortuitously saved from extinction by Cleggy's failure to turn pop star ratings into votes, is now the only national party of opposition. I can't say I am optimistic about the medium-term chances. But here is the rub: has Labour so far lost touch with what it is supposed to be for that it will not be able to rediscover what it is supposed to do? Books such as this are inevitably partly about self-justification, and mine is no exception. So my own experience shows how difficult this process might be, and how wrong I could prove to be.

Too many good people left Labour, and too many good people were blocked because their faces didn't fit. In truth, Labour spent the best part of twenty years eating itself. It then disgorged much of any remaining ability to engage intellectually and lost its ability to connect with working-class voters. It abandoned social democracy, disavowed its history, and turned on some of its most loyal supporters. Many of those who remained in its upper reaches became ever more tribal to compensate, but couldn't quite work out what they were supposed to be tribal about. Since the Labour Party stopped being allowed in effect to choose candidates it really wanted, and since too many of the good people had gone, yet more MPs emerged on the Parliamentary benches who simply waited to be given their orders for the day.

This irks me a good deal less than it once did, because escaping to America was the best thing that I ever did. The idea of having to spend the last several years sitting in a Parliament stuffed to the rafters with on-message, incredibly dull placemen and placewomen fills me with retrospective abject horror. The trouble is, on the Labour side, I know how some of them got there in the first place, and I am still staggered at the low-level chicanery, the venal stupidity and from some of the brighter ones – such as Dr John Reid – the intellectual dishonesty of the New Labour years. Reid, for instance, was often wont to parade Aneurin Bevan in support of his arguments for more privateers in the health service. He also once even managed to invoke Bevan's *In Place of Fear* to justify draconian anti-terror laws at the 2006 Labour Party Conference. This was a device also deployed by Alan Milburn, who ended up advising the Tories on the NHS and getting angry when they backed off from handing the whole thing over to the market.

For some years I sat on the Labour Party's Economic and Social Policy Commission, because Gordon Brown wanted me on it – or at least he had been told to have me on it to keep an eye on me. There was a young woman on the Commission who throughout that whole period never once acknowledged me. She used to look at me with a mixture of revulsion and fear, as though some terrible contagion was about to strike. I later discovered that she had been parachuted into a West Country constituency, where she has since developed a reputation – not as a backbencher who bravely speaks her mind, who stands up on the issues that count, but as an MP who has pioneered the use of 'twitter', who was the first to use her iPhone in the chamber, and other activities of such stunning inanity that it makes your heart bleed.

Recently I watched Ed Miliband on television. Some bright spark had clearly thought that it would be a good idea for him to go and speak to soldiers in Afghanistan, fighting a war without end, a war that almost everyone knows is totally unwinnable and that always has been. Presumably the press officers over at the Foreign Office and the Ministry of Defence muscled in on the act. There he was with his helmet and flak-jacket on, with wee Dougie Alexander to his left, blinking owlishly, and the gawky figure of Shadow Defence Spokesman Jim Murphy to his right.

Everything about the shot was wooden, posed and predictable, and the three of them looked desperately uncomfortable. Never mind that Ed could have used his visit to move away from a bipartisan position of support for the war without end – for starters, neither he or the others looked or sounded right. I called that wise old journalist Geoffrey Goodman, and he agreed that Ed definitely needed some help with his broadcasting skills, as this hadn't been the only TV incident that we had raised our collective eyebrows over. On another occasion, David Cameron had been interviewed in the Cabinet Room, sitting on the edge of the table. The lighting was good, the setting couldn't have been bettered. To some extent it hardly mattered what he may have said. Then they went to Ed. He was in a small, brightly lit room with two shelves behind groaning under the weight of green-bound volumes of Hansard. The lighting was abysmal, the head shot too close – in fact everything about it spelled 'disaster'. If I was a more paranoid character, I might even have thought that it had all been a deliberate set-up.

I wrote to Ed offering to help, and eventually a meeting took place – not with Ed himself but with a couple of his younger advisers, who were both very friendly. It soon became obvious that nothing concrete was going to come of it.

But there was potentially a more important role to play, to bounce ideas off Ed, to help build his confidence and decisiveness, and also to inject some real radical thinking into his leadership.

Frankly, I was a bit insulted that Ed hadn't made the effort to see me. I still can't quite work out though how since becoming leader of the party Ed has had time to see some fifteen or so executives from News International. He was easily trumped by David Cameron who admitted to twenty-six meetings – although he did not admit to what he and they actually talked about. Ed Miliband eventually handled the phone-hacking scandal well, but he and the rest of us owe an enormous debt of gratitude to Labour backbencher Tom Watson for his tenacity.

It struck me that since I had never got involved with the Labour Party at the age of fifteen in order to get a career in politics, it was fairly pointless at the age of forty-eight to go backwards, and once again attempt to find some berth in the Labour Party. Ordinary members may have supported me in droves over the years, and despite my own middle-class background I have always had a good rapport with Labour voters and supporters. What might be thought of as positive advantages are viewed with real fear by the bovine party nomenclature.

The Labour Party has one hell of a way to travel in order to understand just how Blair, Mandelson and in the earlier years

Brown got it all so very wrong. Not just the party, but the MPs and the unions who chose to sit on their hands as the leadership abandoned even the pretence of social democracy, along with four million voters over time. When in the spring of 2011 Labour was displaced by the Scottish Nationalists in its once impregnable heartland of Scotland, the idea that Labour could simply coast back to victory on the back of a Tory-aided economic slump evaporated along with the morning mist.

Ed Miliband is a decent man, who has more depth and a steeliness than his detractors would grant him. Such has been Labour's surrender to free-market fundamentalism over the past fifteen years, the party's current formulaic opposition seems half-hearted and desperately unsure. In 2011, Labour gives every impression of simply not knowing what on earth it stands for, except that it would act more reasonably and sensibly. Given the composition of much of the shadow front bench and the Parliamentary party, it is now extremely difficult for Labour to reconnect with its natural supporters as a party of social democracy, equality of opportunity and redistribution. Ed Miliband finds himself surrounded by unapologetic Blairites, who appear to have learned nothing from Labour's defeat and who give every impression that they would like to replace him at the earliest opportunity.

If there were a New Labour charge sheet, this is how mine would read:

- Opposed the war in Afghanistan from the outset.
- Argued consistently that privatisation had gone too far and that essential services should remain public services.
- Told Gordon Brown that his PFI policy would be a costly mistake for which future generations would pay. Campaigned and voted against it.

- Told GB that Barbara Castle was right – and Labour should restore the State Earnings Related Pension (which he finally did).
- Never believed any of the nonsense peddled about the 'Third Way'(TB) or 'endogenous growth theory'(GB). More to the point, said so and wrote so.
- Argued for tough financial regulation and against further deregulation of financial institutions and the City of London. Didn't think giving the Bank of England independence was particularly radical or a good idea.
- Told Tony Blair he was wrong to block Ken Livingstone from standing as a Labour candidate for Mayor of London. Ditto Rhodri Morgan in Wales. Both of them won consecutive elections, rather proving the point.
- Argued and fought all the way to stop TB taking us to war in Iraq.
- Argued against Britain joining the Single Currency and adopting the European Constitution without a referendum.
- Oh, and argued in the end against abolishing Clause 4 of Labour's Constitution, once I realised what TB's game plan really was: the surrender of social democracy to market forces.

Reading through that charge sheet, I tend to laugh more than cry. Hilariously, many of the numpties that supported TB, PM and GB in whatever they wanted at any particular time are now probably supporting whatever the two Eds, Miliband and Balls, want now. Many of the nomenclature will call this loyalty. I call it unthinking conformity. Others may call it stupidity. 'Blind obedience', wrote Malcolm McLaren of EMI, 'is a sign of stupid fools who stand in line.'

Labour is both intellectually and organisationally weaker than it has been for decades. It stopped thinking for itself a long time ago. Rather than learn from the party's catastrophic defeat, the Blairites unbelievably want to continue with their scorched-earth policy and may yet succeed in grinding Ed Miliband down.

He will need all the support he can get, but he will also need to show that he is prepared to fight a much bigger battle than the one he won against his brother David and the Blairites.

Next Labour

'Rise like Lions after slumber,
In unvanquishable number –
Shake your chains to earth like dew
Which in sleep have fallen upon you –
Ye are many – they are few.'

PERCY BYSSHE SHELLEY, 'The Mask of Anarchy'

IT WAS OF course supposed to be David Miliband as Labour leader, for it had been decreed. More than that, David had the big bucks, he had more Shadow Cabinet members supporting him than all of the other candidates put together. Most of the dreary and predictable commentariat who had acted as cheerleaders for Blair were behind him, largely because the unions were supporting Ed Miliband, and if there is anything that unites much of the commentariat from *The Times* to the *Guardian*, it is a sniffiness towards organised labour and the working class. But even Dennis Skinner was supporting Miliband Major! Now, one shouldn't get too carried away: Dennis essentially thought that there wasn't much difference between the two brothers, but that David was a better performer in Parliament.

On that he may have been right, although I couldn't really remember any stellar performances from Miliband Major, who shared a preference, along with many of his colleagues, for Third Way-type technobabble. Nor, when it came to the leadership campaign, could I personally back him, given his support for the war in Iraq and for his flabbiness over extraordinary rendition.

I had first raised the possibility that extraordinary rendition was taking place in the British Indian Ocean territory of Diego Garcia in the *Independent* back in 2006. A top-ranking former US military commander had admitted that it was going on, but still Foreign Secretary David Miliband denied it all – until he was forced into a humiliating retreat and had to apologise in Parliament.

Miliband Major was described to me, by former Labour backbencher turned Liberal Democrat defector Brian Sedgemore at a long, lugubrious lunch at the National Liberal Club, as 'a kind of robot, assembled in parts out of a packet', which seemed a bit cruel to me.

'If he wins,' said Brian, 'the Daleks will rule the world.' Brian also had some pointed things to day about David's legendary indecisiveness. 'He doesn't like to take risks – a bit like his father Ralph, who was always urging students to rebel and revolt, but when push came to shove was never anywhere to be seen. He was worried about the implications for his pension you see. Father like son.' At the funeral for Ken Coates in Chesterfield, former MEP and veteran troublemaker Hugh Kerr attempted to put me right on the Milibands: 'Ralph always said Labour would betray the working class – and he produced two sons to prove it!' Whereas another Labour veteran in Austin Mitchell said that he couldn't take the Miliband brothers seriously as he remembered changing their nappies.

The claim of indecisiveness was all very well, but I couldn't really blame David for not running against Gordon before the last General

Election when lots of people were urging him to do so. How many of them would risk the withering fire and the 'forces from hell' (to quote Alistair Darling) that Gordon's entourage would have unleashed?

I remember meeting David years back, when John Smith had asked him to go and work for the Borrie Commission on low pay. I can't remember where the suite of offices was, but I do remember meeting David, because he was so obviously nice and other-worldly. I had come to interview Sir Gordon Borrie for *Tribune*, because John Smith had suggested that it would be a good idea, and so there was time for a quick tea from plastic cups with David.

The sands of time have drifted over that particular conversation, but I also used to bump into David in North London for the annual *New Statesman* versus *Tribune* cricket match. As you might expect, the *New Statesman* took all of this horribly seriously, wore whites, and had star players like the journalist and transport expert Christian Wolmar. The *Tribune* team included Chris Smith and Lord Meghnad Desai, who earned the rare and possibly unrepeatable record of being sacked from Labour's front bench twice, and for the same offence. Back in the early 1990s, I had suggested to Meghnad that he take a pop at John Smith and Gordon Brown's new economic policy in *Tribune*, which he duly did. Unfortunately no one had told John Smith, nor had he read *Tribune*, and Smith was ambushed at Prime Minister's Questions. Meghnad was duly fired from his front-bench position in the Lords. Months later he had been rehabilitated by the all-forgiving Smith, and was enjoying himself in his new role as a junior whip, when hey presto! – a Tory peer reprised the same article, quoting from it again. Smith went utterly ballistic at the news, believing that this was a new attack, and Meghnad was duly fired again.

But the *Tribune* team of assorted shabbily-attired ne'er-do-wells also included a rather dashing David Miliband, who in my view could easily have been poached by the *Staggers*. Had he been Blair, of course, he would have gone from the *Staggers* to the *Spectator* as quickly as saying 'knife'.

'David is very easy on the eye!', our production manager Sheila Noble would say, thus proving that David could well have an appeal with ladies of a certain age. And while at my last Labour Party Conference before departing for New York, during a particularly desultory afternoon of set-piece scripted speeches from the 'Speech Writing Unit' to a half-empty hall, a hastily written note arrived via the conference chairman at the top table that looked down at us oiks on the NEC. It was from David Miliband. Although I couldn't read his writing, it seemed to offer some sort of good luck message.

David's enduring problem is that he was once photographed at a Labour conference in Manchester holding a banana in a fairly moronic pose – William Hague's baseball cap moment if you like. In British politics clearly you can survive supporting illegal wars, but being pictured holding a banana is deeply problematic.

Bananas aside, his election as Labour leader would have simply signalled business as usual, and the continuation of the weird cult of New Labour. I decided to do my bit to stop him. I called up Ed Miliband's office and volunteered to go and speak on his behalf. I got a call a week later from someone who sounded about sixteen and was asked to go and 'speak for Ed in Hackney North.'

'Er, but that is Diane Abbott's constituency!', I volunteered – and she was a candidate in the leadership contest.

I called a grown-up. 'Do you really want to entirely piss Diane Abbott off? How stupid is this idea? Wouldn't it be smarter if I went bearing Ed's greetings, praised Diane – and asked the members for their second preference votes for Ed?' I duly turned up to Hackney, sat next to Diane, and made it clear that I was voting for her first – and Ed second. This seemed to flummox former minister Bill

Rammell, who was there to speak for David. But as a tactic it seemed to work, and as a result I found myself making a similar appeal at various left-leaning constituency Labour Parties. On one occasion I was up against the avuncular Charlie Falconer, Blair's old flatmate, who had been gifted a seat in the House of Lords from which much else had flowed. I could see that he has champing at the bit to have a go at me – but what could he do? He was supporting one Miliband, and I was supporting another. Queensbury Rules reigned.

A number of people asked me then and have done so since: 'Why Ed Miliband?' The truth is that I don't really know him, but occasionally used to come across him when he was working as an adviser for Gordon Brown. Quite how he managed to avoid the sheer ghastliness of the Blair-Brown rivalries, I don't know, but that he did so is a recommendation in itself. It was also his good fortune to have been studying for a Fulbright Scholarship when the New Labour government decided to go to war in Iraq. However, others did know him (largely through his father Ralph), most notably the socialist intellectual and former Euro MEP, Ken Coates. Ken had corresponded with Ed, although it was unclear that Ed had replied, principally because he had been close to Ralph Miliband and believed (correctly in my view) that there was far more to Ed than his brother. By 2010, the rump of what was left of the 'thinking Left' had backed Ed Miliband for leader.

His victory in the Labour leadership contest immediately provoked a storm amongst the Blairites and much of the commentariat, with a great deal of criticism being aimed at Labour's electoral college – despite the fact that it was the same electoral college that had elected Tony Blair. What they didn't like was that Ed had won with union support, and in spite of a massive war chest assembled by his brother. And it soon became clear that the Blairites, or New Labourites, were not going to accept the result, and would like Lord Sainsbury to channel cash into various front organisations, rather than give it to the Labour Party.

Neither of the Miliband brothers have the common touch, and they are, like David Cameron and George Osborne, from that curious twilight world of politics and wonkery. They haven't had real jobs and they haven't ever really managed anything. But my gut feeling is that there is more to Ed Miliband than meets the eye, and that he only needs to discover the inner confidence to allow him to stamp his impression on the Labour Party. Politics is a fickle business, and if Ed Miliband doesn't make more of a real impression with voters the knives will be out. Labour's loss of Scotland to the SNP was hardly a good portent for the 2012 London Mayoral elections, although Ed Miliband's summer of strikes against the Murdoch empire hit home – and well. But all the while the irreconcilable Blairites still largely coalesced around Ed's brother, and David appeared not to have given up all hope that the older brother might one day return from across the water. However hard he doth protest, David Miliband has not done the sensible – and obvious – thing and left the Westminster political scene. Instead he is busy exploiting his previous government experience and making a good deal of money while remaining in Parliament. He presides over the shadowy 'Movement For Change', which some are beginning to describe as a 'party within a party'.

'Movement For Change' is run by Miliband's former campaigns manager Blair McDougall, and is engaged in training a new generation of ultra-loyalist activists. Miliband Major's new praetorian guard is not only receiving funding from people who used to give money to the party, but is soliciting it from elsewhere.

Whatever David Miliband's ambitions may or may not be, I realised that there was another reason why he is unlikely ever to replace his brother. I was watching him recently in Parliament, going around shaking hands and generally schmoozing as all serious politicians must do – but only to those that he regarded as 'supporters'. He was giving the cold shoulder to anyone whom he judged may not have been a supporter, thus giving rise to a low rumble from some MPs that he is 'arrogant'. In politics, you have to shake the hands of everyone, whether you like them or not.

Ed Miliband on the other hand is not a natural media performer. Yet during the early months of his leadership he was able to stamp some authority on the party, and in by-elections Labour began the slow and painful process of clawing itself back. The party's lead wasn't strong, and little has emerged that it is original and new. But for a party now thoroughly jaded by the gurus and snake-oil medicine salesmen of the past decade, the emergence of Maurice Glasman, a north London academic and friend of Ed Miliband, did make for an interesting development.

Unusually Glasman, whom Miliband had ennobled, had both hinterland and an appreciation of Labour history, which famously owes more to Methodism than Marx. Cynics might say that it was always going to be easier for Glasman and others of his persuasion to borrow from that part of Labour's largely forgotten history of self help and organisation around community. That said, in an age of market fundamentalism and extreme turbulence there was something altogether meaningful behind the defence of Glasman and others of the ancient rights of the Smithfield porters in the spring of 2011 when set against the real, unaccountable and mediaeval powers of the City of London Corporation. That Labour now inhabits something of a political and intellectual desert is confirmed by the fact that Glasman's essentially small 'c' conservatism reaching out to the forgotten working class comes in the shape of something called 'Blue Labour'.

My hunch is that Labour will eventually be re-radicalised in opposition. It won't take long before the howls of anger and pain from those at the sharp end – Labour's natural constituency – will be heard as the coalition cuts bite ever deeper. And this time the newly insecure and visibly more impoverished middle classes, those who work for less and pay more in taxation in an intended decade-long Tory attempt to claw back the deficit, will become more and more angry. Whereas a quarter of a century ago it was working-class jobs that were going in their hundreds of thousands, taking whole communities to the brink, by the end of the first decade in the twenty-first century middle-class jobs had become increasingly casualised. What is more, salaries and wages had largely failed to keep up with inflation, and increasingly the middle classes, who once imagined that they would be looked after in old age, realised that the old guarantees had gone, along with the index-linked pensions. In all of this, there is a curious historical parallel with the conditions that gave rise to the English Civil War.

The unions may find their voice again, and if their leaders fail to heed it they won't survive. As the United States continues with Keynesian reflation and imposes tariff walls, the Europeans will be forced to follow. And Labour will be able to present voters with a very real choice during the locust years, if it embraces a new economic and environmental internationalism, focussing on creating real jobs and redistributing power and wealth. Inevitably pressure will grow to halt the free movement of labour and capital to the lowest-priced assembly and export platforms, and there may well be increasing demands for selective trade tariffs. For in truth the Western economies are largely being hollowed out before our eyes. Perhaps it may not be too long before China, India and Brazil start introducing quotas for British migrants.

Former Labour premier James Callaghan told the *Daily Mirror*, as others were departing to form the ill-fated SDP in the early 1980s, that the Labour Party had 'very deep roots'. Many of those who formed the SDP, or who went on to take over the Liberal Democrats and also to help create New Labour, tried ultimately to realign British politics on the centre-right – not the centre-left, as they and their media cheerleaders used to claim. Now this tendency are rapidly becoming history. Their tired free-market mantras are played out and finally found wanting, and this section of political establishment is trying to ingratiate itself with David Cameron's Conservatives rather than Ed Miliband's Labour. They hope that yet again history will repeat itself – yet the Blairite interregnum is over. In time Blair himself will be an embarrassing memory, the man himself looking ever more haunted as he flits from continent to continent, always hoping that his plane doesn't break down somewhere rather inconvenient and he is arraigned for trial on war crimes charges.

Tony Blair, the man who had much of the British political and media establishment in thrall to him for the best part of a decade, ended up showing just how vacuous, parochial and shallow much of the establishment was – and is. Even now, Blair's former party and media cheerleaders cannot bring themselves to recognise that the perma-tanned, ageing figure before them is a shallow actor who dragged Britain into an illegal war, and who ended up grubbing for cash. The man who was serenaded into Downing Street to the sound of 'Things can only get better' ended up giving empty homilies for cash to organisations such as the North American Sanitary Ware Association.

From this point at least, things can at long last begin to get better. Well they must, mustn't they?

Endpiece

'For really I think that the poorest he that is in England hath a life to live, as the greatest he.'

THOMAS RAINSBOROUGH, Leveller, Republican and English Revolutionary, in the Putney Debates, 1647.

BACK IN 1989, my wife Yasmin and I went to Prague. We were staying with Czech dissident friends on Avenue Leninova, where the trolleybuses went clanking past below. Perhaps a former Charles University Professor was driving one, or could it even have been Jiri Dienstbier? Dientsbier later became the first Foreign Minister of a free Czechoslovakia after the fall of Communism in 1989, famously being picked up outside the factory he was working in by a government car to be whisked off to the Foreign Ministry to begin his new job.

Communist hegemony was already beginning to crack as we flew into Prague, the thaw having come at the behest of Mikhail Gorbachev, a leader who still dwarfs all those who have followed in his wake into the Kremlin. But Prague then was still in deep winter, presided over by party boss Miroslav Stephan, the sort of bully-boy ignoramus who tends to thrive as politics stagnates and the system atrophies. Stephan was feared, not only by the friends we were staying with, who had been delighted when we had arrived bearing gifts of copies of *The Times* and the *Guardian*, but by many others. Yet the rabble-rousing, anti-Semitic Stephan, along with the Czech secret police, the STB and the whole Communist edifice, was about to be shaken to the core. For by the time we had arrived, hordes of holidaying East Germans were queuing to get out of the now open borders of *glasnost*-affected Hungary in their two-stroke Trabants. That also meant that the escaping East Germans were using Czechoslovakia as part of the freedom route to the West.

We were there on that first major demonstration against the party bosses in Wenceslas Square. Elderly people at first, holding aloft yellowing newspapers featuring Alexander Dubcek, leader of the Prague Spring. Then more joined them, and more and more. And soon the square was full of people shouting 'Dubcek! Dubcek!', even though Brezhnev's tanks had crushed the Czech bid for freedom in 1968 and Dubcek was a forbidden name.

The demonstration couldn't last, of course. First came the buses full of 'workers militia', hired thugs from the factories, and then came the riot police, batons raised, on horseback. Young students were baton-charged and thrown into waiting vans. A nearby church was invaded and protestors dragged out screaming. One of the protestors had thrown Yasmin a roll of film, shouting, 'Take the pictures – and show the world!'

We never saw Dubcek. That drama was to come later, after we had returned to Britain, when he finally joined Vaclav Havel to wave from the balcony at the crowds below that had filled Wenceslas Square now that the STB and Stephan's thugs had melted away.

Dubcek was a reluctant, self-effacing leader, an earlier reformist version of Gorbachev. His misfortune was his timing, while facing an entrenched power elite that saw any challenge as one to be crushed. Unlike Imre Nagy, the leader of the Hungarian revolt of 1956, Dubcek wasn't killed after Brezhnev sent the Russian tanks rumbling in across the cobbles. He was exiled to Bratislava and spent the next two decades as a humble forestry worker.

In Britain, we do not have a habit of crushing protests with tanks, still less killing or imprisoning political opponents. In Britain we like to believe that we are a liberal democracy which not only tolerates dissent but encourages it. But ask yourself this: where are the dissenters today, except at the margins where they can be safely patronised and policed? Where are the brave newspaper editors prepared to risk all to stand up for something, anything? Where are the political leaders who dare to challenge orthodoxy and who dare to think original thoughts and construct arguments around them? In our increasingly tattered, threadbare democracy, where intellect and independent thought is frowned on, humour regarded with suspicion and anything beyond the narrow consensus viewed as 'extremism', there is less and less wriggle room for non-conformists instead we asked to celebrate the infantalisationn of our post-ideological age.

It is hardly surprising then that the political class is not just disliked, it is widely detested. Despite this reality, we can observe growing confidence on the part of a very old English establishment that has never truly relinquished its hold. It has succeeded in 'rolling back the state', rolling back the unions, and rolling back many of the post-war gains. Having quashed its opponents in the factories and workplaces during the 1980s and largely absorbed the Labour Party into its embrace, this establishment is justly confident that its wealth and power are firmly entrenched and protected. Two-tier Britain – the super-rich and the rest of us – becomes more permanent, utterly unhindered, for there is no longer any real opposition to it from any powerful quarter. In today's Britain the rich just keep getting so much richer. The bankers and City spivs who drove the

economy to a precipice emerge unscathed and can occasionally be found sheltering behind the new device of the super-rich: the super injunction. Elsewhere the legal profession, teaching and almost every other facet of professional life where the poor and the middling had made some modest gains is once again dominated by the sons and daughters of the wealthy. The middle classes now find themselves in a similar position as the working class back in the 1980s, unsure of their jobs and aware that their children will be paying the debts of the boomer generation for decades to come, now that the latter have kicked the ladder away.

And as the first decade of the twenty-first century ended it was fast becoming apparent that the ordinary people of these islands were being forced to pay in their jobs and taxes for the greed of the bankers, the deindustrialisation and pauperisation of an economy. The few real gains of the previous century, most notably the National Health Service, stood on the brink of being cherry-picked by the private sector. In truth, over the preceding quarter-century most of the state assets of any worth had been sold off for a song, as successive governments worshipped at the feet of the 'free market'. Britain's industrial and productive base had been deliberately run down in favour of the 'service sector' and the financial services industry, which was in itself cushioned by the consensus view that 'light touch regulation' is best. And looking around, it was striking to see how little opposition there had been to all of this from the horribly weakened unions and from a party that had gone from being Labour to New Labour to Invisible Labour. Victorian times had returned with a vengeance, perhaps answering Margaret Thatcher's seemingly ludicrous wish at the time for the return of 'Victorian values'. And the Conservative Party that had seemingly left Eton and the grouse moors behind with Alec Douglas Home had produced a shiny new protean Etonian leader, one who had the nerve to deride those who were still disgusted by the regression of Britain into the super-rich and the poor as 'dinosaurs'.

Meanwhile the pretence that this increasingly youthful political class actually knew what it was doing was maintained. This despite the fact that few politicians had ever had real jobs or knew anything much about the real world. And this at the same time that an altogether newer and pervasive culture of graft and corruption became more established in public life. In the dying days of the previous century and the early days of this, many national and local politicians in cahoots with some senior public servants came to believe that they too were entitled to join the benefits culture of the super-rich. They fiddled their expenses and they promoted one another to various sinecures, milking the system while scapegoating those at the bottom of the pecking order. Once upon a time, ordinary British voters were wont to say come election time that 'They're all in it together!' without really being able to define what 'it' was. By the end of the first decade of the twenty-first century, not only did people know exactly what 'it' was, they really knew that the political class were all in it together. They probably knew also that the 'political parties' they were periodically asked to vote for were largely empty shells.

In my own small way I ran up against the guns and am here to tell this tale. This is England, after all. But as I ponder what to do next – or perhaps more to the point what I may be allowed to do – I do think of Alexander Dubcek in his Bratislavan forest, for my experience in Britain, in a much smaller way, has its similarities. I know that this may chime for many others who have refused in their own different ways to toe the line, who continue to question authority and to stake out territory of which the political and media establishment does not approve.

Not that this should dissuade the next generation of dissenters for one minute.